Strangers i

Strangers in the Pews

*The Pastoral Care of Psychiatric Patients
within the Christian Congregation*

Roger Grainger

EPWORTH PRESS

For Stuart Brand

0 7162 0494 0

First published 1993
by Epworth Press
1 Central Buildings, Westminster, London SW1H 9NR

Phototypeset by Selwood Systems, Midsomer Norton
Printed in Finland by
Werner Söderström Oy

Contents

Preface

Christians have always been under the obligation to make friends with strangers. God sent his Son into a hostile world: Jesus was bound to be a stranger, even though he shares our humanity. He was bound to be a stranger *because* he shares our humanity. Being a stranger was the job he had to do, the mission he had to perform. Strangerhood belonged to his humanity as well as his divinity.

We still have a lot of strangers, and they need their representatives; to be a stranger is to be human. The strangers we must welcome are not only strange to ourselves personally, they are sometimes strangers to our community. Sometimes they are strange to society as a whole. This book is about people who come into our lives, our congregations, our society, from outside. They are the 'strangers in our pews'. During the last fifteen years or so, the centuries-old practice of shutting up – encarcerating – mentally disturbed and mentally handicapped people in mental hospitals has given way to a policy of widespread hospital closure, and the resettlement of patients in local neighbourhoods, where they can live under the same social conditions as everyone else. The strangers in our pews are strangers not only to the congregation of the local church, but to the social networks from which the congregation is made up. This is the main area of difference – the fact of a number of years spent shut away from the world, a number of years learning the identity of a mental patient. The people from the hospital are not so strange in themselves; the strangeness has come from other people who, over the centuries have, in the words of the hymn, 'made strange and refused to know' them. Those who do get to know them usually find the experience rewarding. Christians, being outcasts themselves – at least when they are *most* themselves, most faithful to the gospel – ought to recognize the special needs of outcasts. Because they themselves, as Christians, have known what it is to be considered strange, they should be willing to listen and to learn, so that strangeness can give way to sharing and sharing to joy. This book came from my own experience, both as a psychiatric patient and as a chaplain working amongst mentally disturbed people. I am sure that the way towards life within the community is, for many, acceptance within the community of Christ. I am equally sure that we, as Christians, can only benefit and grow wiser and more compassionate from what patients and ex-patients have to teach us – things that it seems society cannot yet bear to hear. The wisdom of Hebrews is there to remind us: 'Remember always to welcome strangers, for by doing this some people have entertained angels unawares' (Heb. 13.2).

Introduction

With the closure of the old mental hospitals the church has found itself dragged into contact with mental disability in a way, and to an extent, that has not been the case since the Reformation. During this psychiatric revolution successive governments have handed over the care of disturbed people to non-statutory bodies within the community to an extent previously undreamed of. Foremost among such agencies, of course, has been the church. This book attempts to make this new burden of responsibility a little easier to bear for the clergy and lay people concerned – and through them, for the thousands of ex-patients who have been 'decanted' into the community and are trying to find a new way of life apart from the hospital.

One of the ways I hope to do this, however, is to paint a picture of mental illness and mental handicap which is less negative than the usual one. It seems to me that the events of the last twenty years present the churches with an opportunity to fulfil their mission of love and deliverance to all mankind. 'All mankind' in this case includes the most stigmatized and rejected section of society – hardly a section of society at all because it has been specifically excluded. The matter of its re-inclusion, of the re-personalization of its inhabitants is on offer to any individual or group of individuals able or willing to take it up. Surely the church will try to respond to such a challenge.

The danger, however, is that the clergy will be too unsure of themselves to think about rising to the occasion. They are

not psychiatrists or psychiatric social workers. It is not their
job to be able to deal with mental illness or mental handicap.
If they try to do what they are not trained to do they may
very well make things worse. Besides, in all conscience they
have enough on their plate coping with their own fold, apart
from *themselves*. At this point, they groan as if to say, 'I'm
the one who really needs help.'

Perhaps they do – but not in the way they mean. Clergy
need help in making use of the skills they've got: skills of love,
patience and understanding; intuition and acceptance of other
people as other and yet, at the deepest level, so very like
oneself. These skills, which are shared and improved on by
the congregation, are the ones you need for re-personalizing
oppressed and disorientated people. If you feel you need to
learn about mental illness and handicap from a psychiatric
point of view you would probably be advised to listen to a
psychiatrist who would supply the common sense lacking in
so many books on the subject. You will certainly need specialist help with someone who is distressed in a way that continues
to resist every effort you make to calm them. Most of the
time, however, you and your congregation are more effective
than any psychiatrist. What you can give is a sense of the
meaning of life as this is discovered, in the experience of God's
love. It is meaning and love that transforms patients into
people. I promise that if you stick with it, you will find out
for yourselves.

I

Getting Involved

That house from down the road, the one that's been empty,
Have you seen the people who've just moved in?
No, I haven't seen them yet, either –
But I've heard about them. They're from *that place* –
Yes, that one –
THE ASYLUM
(Well, I don't care, that's what it is,
that's what it always has been,
you know as well as I do!)
I don't know what you think, but I don't think it's right.
I know they've got to live somewhere, and I'm sure I
wouldn't like to have to spend my life in that place,
But it's what they're used to, after all, and I'm sure they're
much happier there.
It's a 'safe environment', isn't it?
Because you can say what you like, they're not the same as
us,
And we shouldn't expect them to be, it wouldn't be fair –
Not fair on them, I mean.
I'm only thinking of them, after all.
I want them to be happy; as happy as people like that can
be, I mean.
(I really don't know what's happening to this neigh-
bourhood, what with the Sikh Temple, and Mrs Williams's
coloured lodger, and now these;
such a nice house, no. 39 –
What a pity!)

This is a book about the church and mental disability. The problem of caring for mentally ill and mentally handicapped people continues, whether they are housed on hospital wards or live in houses specially set aside for them in a particular town or suburb. Since the large hospitals began to close down, things have become more complicated than they used to be. Nowadays those who need psychiatric help are scattered throughout the neighbourhood instead of living together in one place. This can be much better for them, or it can be much worse: better if it works out all right, worse if it doesn't. The failure of the new policy and the terms on which it might succeed are things to be discussed later on.

For the time being, however, many of the old hospitals remain partly in use, looking after people who are too old or too ill to be expelled, and giving temporary shelter to those who are acutely disturbed and must go somewhere away from family and friends until the crisis has passed. Only in a minority of cases has governmental policy been carried out to the letter, usually where the local general hospitals have themselves opened psychiatric wards.

All this makes the church's job more difficult. Pastoral care takes place now in a wide variety of settings – group homes, where ex-patients live together as families, hostels where they stay for a limited time before moving on, drop-in centres, half-way houses, bedsits, flats, bed and breakfast hotels on the one hand; psychiatric wards in general hospitals, community clinics, wards in half- or three-quarters-closed asylums on the other. On one level, however, it stays the same. This is the basic level of reaching out to the mentally ill, sustaining a relationship with all their various worlds. The division is not between hospital and community but between what we regard as sanity and what we call madness. I may have as little contact with the young housewife who has turned her face to the wall of the community clinic as I had with the old gent knocking at the third floor window of the old psychiatric hospital.

At another level, one which is equally important, if I am a minister I may find myself having more contact with mental illness than I ever had before. And I may find this alarming. Certainly there is more need for pastoral care now than ever before. Whatever may be said about the asylums, they were at least safe. Such was their intention, to keep the insane and the sane apart, thus providing security for both. This was the job that they had done so successfully for almost two hundred years. Now that the wards are closed and the corridors rapidly gathering dust there remains nothing to protect each side from the other. So long as we tell ourselves that modern psychiatric treatment is able to eliminate any signs of illness, so that patients and ex-patients can be considered to be exactly the same as everybody else, there is nothing to worry about. Unfortunately, however, this is obviously not the case. Firstly, people who are psychiatrically ill aren't able to choose when and where to break down. Secondly, even if they do manage to have their injections and take their tablets regularly, there really isn't much chance that they will ever be treated as quite normal, however ordinary their behaviour may be. Medication which works psychiatrically still manages to fail socially – 'He's on tablets, you know!'. Ex-patients can suffer from stigma just as much as the hospitals they used to call home. More in fact, because their presence is more intrusive. They are actually here, living amongst us, coming to our services!

On the other hand, the over-riding impression I have received of people who are psychiatrically ill is that they feel that other people consider them to be unworthy. Mental illness acts as an indelible stain on a person's self-esteem so that they feel outlawed from the ordinary world of ordinary people. They may not always feel like this, but it is always there in the back of their minds, waiting to be touched off by any suggestion, however slight, that others regard them as patients rather than people. When they are feeling particularly rejected there is a tendency for patients and ex-patients to wear their stigmatized condition with an air of distinction: I can't be *like* you, but you have to admit that I'm a hell of a lot more interesting than you are! This is a natural kind of defensiveness, in some ways a healthy response to the almost inevitable reductiveness of outsiders' attitudes. We must try to be prepared for this, and find ways through to the real hurt, the underlying sensitivity, in order to try and relieve its pain.

In fact nobody likes to admit to the presence of stigma. People who are not themselves stigmatized will tell you that it no longer exists, that it went out with the Mental Health Act in 1957, when the gates of the old asylums were thrown open and the number of locked wards drastically reduced. Many patients at this time were given the option of leaving hospital. These were people no longer considered to be ill, along with some who had been admitted years before and had in fact never been ill. They had been rejected by their families and had simply nowhere else to go. Some left, many chose to stay. At the same time the iron lock had been shattered and the spell that held these hospitals in their own unique institutional limbo for over a century was, at last, lifted.

The stigma did not die, however; I suppose stigma rarely does. It simply became more mobile; now it followed patients out through the gates, clinging to them wherever they went, often for the rest of their lives. I believe that it is true to say that the opening of the mental hospitals actually moved their stigma out into the community, by making it clear that it was not mental hospitals but mentally ill people who were the principal objects of social disdain. The hospitals had at least served the purpose of containing mental illness; keeping it, and those who had it, safely away from contact with normal everyday life. In the real world outside the gate they were used as a way of terrifying naughty children – apart from that they could be forgotten, and mental illness with them.

No chance of forgetting it now, however. When hospital

closure became the policy of successive governments the problem of stigma reasserted itself in ways that had not been seen for two hundred years. There is no need to go into details; most people are only too aware of it. Wherever there is a hospital for mentally ill or mentally handicapped people there are disputes as to whether or not particular areas are suitable for group homes or hostels. Americans, who are even more familiar with the phenomenon having come across it earlier, call it 'nimby'-ism: 'not in my back yard'. It is one of the reasons why ex-patients often have nowhere to live.

It is, after all, only human to take account of what others think of you. Indeed there would be neither family life nor civilization if we didn't do this. At the same time, to take too much notice of other people's negative judgments is to run the risk of becoming estranged from oneself as well as from them. G. H. Mead, the great American social psychologist, called this 'taking the role of the other': looking at ourselves from the outside as if we were someone else. Everybody needs to be able to do this, of course, but those who have managed to develop a robust sense of identity are able not to allow themselves to be too greatly influenced by the messages that they pick up from others. It is, after all, entirely possible, or even likely, that I know more about my real self than other people do, and that my own experience is more authentic than the picture they try to sell me. If I am unsure of myself to begin with, however, I am only too liable to latch on to any negative judgments I can find and incorporate them into my own view of myself, making it progressively worse.

Broadly speaking, it is in this area of life that the problem of mental illness exists. Whatever may be the causes of various forms of mental illness, the results always concern a person's view of his or her self and the world she or he lives in. It is, in effect, a breakdown of the ability to relate. There is a tendency among psychiatric patients to be sensitive to criticism of any kind. I tend to think of it as a kind of fragility – as if somebody had been stripped of their protective skin, the various layers of experience and understanding which allowed them to be sure of themselves in the company of other people. Whether it is their illness or their circumstances, mentally ill people are in an exceptionally vulnerable position. Real rejection, actual hostility, the kind of attitude and behaviour that so often exist towards mentally ill people within society, is likely to hurt its victims so much more than it would so-called 'sane' people. The last thing they need is for their own distorted views of themselves to be reinforced by the reality of other people's unkindness.

Our job as ministers of word and sacrament is to work towards greater acceptance and understanding of people caught in the social trap which exists between being shut up and forgotten, tidied away by the rest of humanity, and really integrated within the community, incorporated along with their fellow men and women in the public and private life of the community. One way or another we must try to create relationships and improve attitudes; to build bridges across a wide river of misunderstanding and fear. We will often fail: the river flows swiftly and has carved a very deep channel. Nevertheless, we can't ignore it. Those who are willing to take up a position on one side or the other are only avoiding the issue.

This kind of bridge-building has to be started from the middle and worked outwards. Our job is to plunge in and lay the first stone. In other words it is precisely the kind of thing that we find ourselves doing so often in our kind of work. The only difference is that the lines of demarcation are usually somewhat clearer. St Paul tells us that 'God was in Christ, reconciling the world to himself' (II Cor. 4.19). The business of reconciliation is the very heart of the new creation. Every Christian, ordained or not, is devoted to it and draws life from it. This is the kingdom we work towards and the way we work towards it. Perhaps we should remind ourselves of the hardships associated with it, and remember the cost involved, the price paid by builders of bridges – 'the life laid down for others to pass over'. I suggest we do so for purposes of understanding rather than comparison, in case we fall into the trap of over-valuing our own contribution. It is Christ who has paid the price for us, and it is his life we share, both the glory and the pain – but more importantly the glory ...

'In Jesus, the Son of God, we have the supreme high priest who has gone through to the highest heaven' (Heb. 4.14). Our job is to set forward the purposes of reconciliation, mediation and celebration. There's a lot of joy in this job. Once the river has been bridged, there is the opportunity for friendship as contact leads to understanding, and under-standing becomes involvement, and sometimes love. Certainly there is no love for us without involvement – the meeting and sharing that takes place when over and over again, right in the middle of whatever it is we happen to be doing at the time, the Word becomes flesh.

As Christians we know that whenever we celebrate Jesus' life, death and resurrection we assert our own identity as sharers in his reconciling work. This happens time and again, as part of our daily and weekly routine, although for us it is never mere routine. The Spirit we invoke is the Spirit of new life, fresh beginnings, meaning bestowed upon the past, the hope of understanding, breaking through and changing the dilemmas of the present. Certainly this is evidence of our joy as Christians. We do it in unexpected places and at unorthodox times, formally and informally, so that people wonder what it is that we are doing and we can invite them to 'come and see'. Building bridges is the characteristic action of our ministry to the mentally ill and disabled and those with learn-ing difficulties. And yet, the obstacle is basically the same wherever we are. It is the space 'between man and man'. In other words, it is humanity faced with the demand of God, the God who confronts us in relationships. There can be no relationship without separation, no experience of meeting without individuals who break through to it by reaching across to each other. God is to be encountered precisely here, where communication is most difficult.

The other great attraction of working among mentally ill people is the people themselves. This is a considerable privilege. Some people talk about psychiatric patients as if they were pieces of machinery whose control centres had developed some kind of malfunction. What I have to say in the following pages is not likely to make sense to these people. Others tend to regard them as intrinsically different from themselves, organized on totally different lines: 'If I don't understand them, they can't possibly be understood.' The trouble with this kind of personal withdrawal is that it leads to a kind of determination *not* to understand. The next step is superstitious dread, as of something totally 'beyond the pale', whose presence is intolerable, whose existence is a threat to our tried and tested arrangements for living.

Those who come into frequent contact with people using psychiatric services tend to see things in another way. Their views of mental illness will be rather different from other people's largely because they happen to know some mentally ill people. Knowing real people is all the difference in the world from picking up someone else's ideas (or lack of ideas) about them. I said earlier that understanding led to involvement, but this is not always the order in which it happens. In my own experience I have usually found that involvement comes first, and then understanding. I have been drawn towards somebody by the intensity of their distress or the challenge of my own inability to communicate; and out of this has come a quality of relationship which leads to a measure of understanding. It may only be a glimmer. Nevertheless it can lead to a kind of loving. This, again, is a kind of bridge-building, perhaps the most basic and essential kind so far as our relationship with patients is concerned. It is by no means all one way. It couldn't work if it were. A minister or a priest is important to the business of healing not because of what he or she does, but because of what he or she is. Our presence draws attention to a different kind of meaning, one that affects the meaning of the entire enterprise. Sometimes this may be resented, but I get the impression that in a strange way it is often appreciated by those who have no religious beliefs themselves. From one point of view, of course, we have a very definite function – that of the 'joker in the pack', the medically naive person concerned with people rather than illnesses. It never does us any harm to know something about illness, of course, so long as people associate us with health. We are part of their ordinary day-to-day living, in which we depend on one another rather than on the skilled intervention of professionals. Our very existence is a kind of criticism of a system that depends entirely upon human ability to control events. It refers to an awareness of spiritual meanings which abide in the background of life, an unexplored dimension of experience which cannot safely be ignored. The priest or minister is a kind of memento hominorum – a reminder of our identity as creatures of God, finally and inexorably dependent upon him for our very being. We have more authority than we know!

2

Simply People

They are rebuilding the semi-detached house next door to the drop-in centre in Station Road. The local Association for Mental Health has managed to get hold of it so that they can extend their premises. In a sudden, unexpected access of generosity, the council have not only forgone the rent on Number 12 for another year, but have decided to throw in Number 14 as well. At the moment a gang of volunteers of every age and size is poking boards through empty windows and dislodging chunks of plaster on to the pavement, spurred on by the thought of being able to have a proper lounge to relax in, plus a separate games room. The two houses are in the process of being knocked into one, so there will be exactly twice as much room as there was previously. The tall woman in dungarees, her face smeared where she has wiped sweat off and paint on, is Jill, the part-time unpaid semi-official warden of the project. Jill is both a user of the mental health services and a provider of them, having been involved in the negotiations leading up to the present chaos, which she views with obvious satisfaction. The tidily-dressed man standing next to her is Tom. He is not so pleased. The extensions mean that the centre will go on being closed for several weeks. 'I don't see why *both* houses have to be out of commission: you're only working on the new one!' Unfortunately, however, there are doorways to be knocked in the party wall, at least one room to be extended, and a porch either demolished or extended. All of which takes time, so Tom must wait. It's not as if he's going anywhere!

This, however, is precisely the point. Tom isn't going anywhere. He has plenty of time, more than he can cope with.
Plenty of time and nothing to do. Coming to the day centre
is all he does at present. It is his spiritual lifeline, the meaning
of his day. Since he came out of hospital six months ago he
has depended more and more on the drop-in centre for the
support he needs. He doesn't do much when he's there, just
sits in an easy chair with his legs crossed and pretends to
smoke his pipe. (Tom gave up smoking several years ago but
he can't bear to be without the briar his wife gave him shortly
before she died.) On a good day he'll talk wisely about the
meaning of life and the futility of religion – being careful
always to spare the feelings of those who don't share his
opinions. The sitting room looks bare without him. People
who are engaged in keeping cheerful complain that his presence depresses them, which is unfair because he always takes
great care to respect people's feelings and keeps silent when
he is feeling sad.

Which, unfortunately tends to be often. Since his wife died
Tom has been admitted to hospital four times, diagnosed as
suffering from reactive depression – in other words, extreme
grief leading to repeated attempts at suicide. For six months
he has made his way every Monday, Wednesday and Friday
to Station Road to meet his friends. On Wednesday evenings
he helps run a group designed to help users and ex-users with
emotional problems. Although he has never had any formal
training, he is a natural counsellor and his work is very much
appreciated. If you were to ask him his opinion about the
drop-in centre he would tell you that it had changed his life:
'I only wish Phyllis could meet these people. If only she were
here to see how wonderful they are.' After he has said this he
doesn't say anything else for a long time.

The drop-in centre provides a vital service for a good many
in the town. People who have been in psychiatric hospitals,
or are having psychiatric treatment at home, are very lonely
people indeed. Sometimes this is because other people go out

of their way to avoid them, crossing over the street so as not to have to talk to them. Whether this is because they are terrified by the idea of mental illness, or frightened that to intervene would make the patient feel worse, the effect is the same: greater loneliness and rejection, more evidence in support of the growing conviction of personal unworthiness founded in the experience of the illness itself. At the drop-in centre you can talk naturally to other people, just as if you were not a pariah. At the drop-in centre, for a couple of hours a day, you can inhabit the real world.

During the last six months of his stay at Western Meads Hospital, Philip used to practise regularly, picking up the church key from the porter's lodge. It was a remarkable organ, regularly tuned by the hospital authorities and a joy to play on, despite the fact that the dampness of the church had certainly taken its toll in the century since it was first installed. The hospital legend claimed that it had once been played by Sir Edward Elgar himself on a visit to a member of staff who had been a member of Elgar's silver band at Powicke Hospital. Whether or not this was true, Philip liked to imagine that Elgar's spirit was still wandering around the fragrant wood-work ... A month before he was discharged he discovered a copy of Elgar's organ sonata on a market stall. Fascinated by what he had found he went straight back to the church and began to practise. Although largely self-taught, Philip was a good organist, well on the way to being a brilliant one; this was the music he needed and he certainly did it justice ...

When he left the hospital he moved into a flat in a small town about five miles away. He was living apart from his wife at this time. His changes of mood made him a hard person to live with. It was Patricia's decision that she had had more than she could stand that had given rise to the outbreak of real mental illness that had brought him into hospital. By profession he was a teacher, although that, like his marriage, had suffered as a result of his emotional instability. After having five jobs in four years, Philip had given up the idea of being a teacher and joined the queue at the Labour Exchange. Those who knew him, including at least three of his headmasters, would have thought this a great waste of talent, and not only musical talent but ability as a teacher, too. When he was good, Philip was very good indeed.

The trouble lay in the times when he was not good. Philip suffered from manic depression. This meant that for long periods of time at a stretch, sometimes up to three or four months, all he would feel was grief at being alive. From time to time this would intensify to become a real desire for death. During the three years preceding entry into Western Meads Philip made five suicide attempts. In between these times he was happy and worked hard. Harder than most, in fact; to see Philip on a good day was to be cheered and inspired. People who knew him in both his moods were puzzled by the contrast. Perhaps if he didn't throw quite so much of himself into things he wouldn't get such a terrible reaction, they said.

Somehow the sonata represented his rediscovered health. He began to think about teaching again. In the meantime he looked round for somewhere to practise ... The parish church seemed rather formal, if not pompous. He wanted somewhere quieter. He found a church on the edge of town which seemed just right; the organ was good, too. Full of confidence, he introduced himself to the minister. 'Where are you from?' said the minister, whose name was Simon, and Philip told him. The minister seemed interested: 'Do you feel you can make your home among us?' As a matter of fact he was genuinely pleased to have an ex-patient in his congregation. He had a lot of sympathy for people like that.

Philip was pleased as well. He liked the church and he liked the minister. He liked the organ too, and longed to play it. As a newcomer, however, he hesitated to ask. People were friendly but not too friendly – definitely a neighbourhood where they 'kept themselves to themselves'. He wondered how many knew where he had spent the last four months. He was puzzled, wanting to know more about people, but feeling inhibited by the general atmosphere of politeness. Simon was puzzled, too. He felt he should be doing something to help the young man settle down. Why had he come here? There was much more going on at the parish church in the town.

One Saturday afternoon Simon came into the church when Philip was playing the organ. He had finally summoned the courage to ask the organist if he might practise on Saturday afternoons. The organist said that he had no objection at all. An elderly man, he seemed delighted that Philip had asked him – he didn't know how long it had been since anyone showed any interest in the organ. He said he would tell the minister but forgot to do so. Philip was playing the Elgar when Simon came into the church. He waited until Philip had finished, sitting down in the choir stalls. 'I had no idea you could play like that,' he said. 'Well, you don't really know very much about me, do you?' said Philip.

It would be hard to say which played the greater part in Philip's rehabilitation, the lithium carbonate or St Michael's. He had to keep on with both; he couldn't afford to give either of them up. By 'rehabilitation' I mean his 're-introduction to ordinary life'. Philip was still manic depressive. He still suffered from recurrent changes of mood which ordinary human determination was powerless to control: what he described as 'the failure of my pull-yourself-together bit'. It didn't take long for the congregation at St Michael's to notice that Philip had 'bad days'. Philip himself made no attempt to cover up the fact of his illness; indeed, it seemed to help him to talk about it. What wasn't so obvious, and had to be learned over the years, was that it was during the times of depression, when Philip was most unapproachable, that he most needed company; not to try to jolly him out of his mood – that only made things worse – but simply to be with him as a gesture of love and friendship. This did not result in any appreciable change of mood; at the same time, at the very deepest level of all, it was profoundly appreciated.

When the organist retired Philip took over from him. Simon wasn't quite sure whether he should permit this. Wouldn't it be too great a strain? What would happen if (he meant 'when') he was depressed? On those Sundays when his feelings got the better of him during the service Philip was in the habit of leaving as unobtrusively as possible. He couldn't do that if he was playing the organ, could he? Perhaps it would be a good idea if he had a six-month trial period 'to see how things turned out'. Philip was only too pleased to agree to this. Nobody was more aware of his drawbacks than he was. He's still playing the organ. It gives him something to cling to when he's down. In the meantime he has become one of the most celebrated church organists in the area. As yet he hasn't been known to walk out.

(Some months ago he was invited to play the organ at the cathedral. He played the Elgar Sonata and received an ovation. Next week at St Michael's he was asked to play it again but was much too depressed to do so. Perhaps the 'high' triggered off the 'low'; perhaps he was due for a period of depression according to the cycle of his mood swings. Whichever it was, it was lived through with a bit of help from his friends . . .)

Philip's story calls to mind one of the main difficulties involved in coping with that aspect of people we know, love and appreciate which concerns mental illness. Although he was suffering from a mental illness, Philip needed to be treated as normal. If you are a disabled person you find yourself on the horns of a dilemma. First of all you want and need help from other people – you can't live among them properly unless you can live like them, which means being as free from pain and as independent as possible. Independence, however, means *not* needing help – you need help in order not to need it. Disabled people feel considerably reduced by being reminded by others of their disability. On the other hand, they obviously cannot cope with the expectations made of the un-disabled, and resent the implication that they should have to do so. To be disabled is to live between the scylla of frustration and the charybdis of humiliation. This is true of emotional and cognitive disabilities as well as physical ones. Individual women and men may not always behave as though they are aware of the pressure of this double-bind on their lives, but there is no way in which they can avoid situations in which they resent having to ask for the help they need. Particularly if the problem is psychiatric.

Another thing that Philip's story illustrates is the slippery nature of mental illness as a category. The fact is that it isn't a useful way of thinking about mental illness to regard it as totally different from what we are accustomed to call sanity. The churches are full of people who are 'abnormal'. Indeed, it would be an impoverished congregation without people whom psychiatrists did not consider to be predisposed to one form of madness or another. Philip is an example of somebody actually diagnosed as suffering from psychosis who appeared perfectly normal for most of the time. Not only appeared but *was* – it was only during a down-swing that Philip's experience and behaviour became pathological in any sense of the word. Somebody whose disability concerned thinking rather than feeling might be even more difficult to distinguish from a parishioner who had become eccentric as a result of living alone for a long time. Judgments about mental health are never easy, even for professionals.

How, then, should we treat men and women who are suffering from mental illness? Are they just like ourselves, only psychologically damaged and needing more care, a greater effort of understanding on our part? Should we treat them like everyone else, but with more than usual circumspection? If so, how much more? More to the point, circumspection about what? Clergy are not psychiatrists. They can't be expected to be au fait with the kinds of things that should be avoided in their relationships with people suffering from mental illness. This really does constitute a problem in community care. Almost everybody is very worried about this. What if we make things worse by doing the wrong thing?

I firmly believe that it is better to err on this side than the other. Doing the wrong thing is preferable to doing nothing at all. The right thing is to ask the person concerned what it is that they find difficult to cope with and see what can be done about it. Get them to talk to you about their symptoms, so that you can see things through their eyes. If you don't see the world their way, tell them so; but make it clear that you respect the fact that *they* do and that you value their experience. Don't be nervous about this. You won't catch anything! These are real people, not figures of fantasy from the attics of our nightmares. Any contagion they possess they have caught from us. It is our attitude that turns them into lepers.

When Philip was too depressed to go and see his psychiatrist Simon persuaded him to go by offering to go with him. The second time he did this he managed to have a word with the psychiatrist, who was very pleased that Philip had attached himself to St Michael's: 'Not only a church but an organ as well.' He explained to Simon that people suffering from manic depression were often extremely creative, producing a great deal of good work when in their 'manic' phase – that is, the periods of activity and energy which alternate with depression to form 'manic depression'. Sometimes people are more manic than they ever are depressed, and this is always very hard on their friends and relatives who may find themselves being 'run off their feet' and involved in all sorts of wild schemes, but when someone's mood swings tend towards periods of real depression, their manic phase may express itself in ideas and activities that are imaginative but realistic. Philip was a good example of this. Was he a good organist?

Simon said he was the best that the church had ever had. The consultant said he was not a bit surprised. Many of the world's most creative artists had been manic depressives: Michelangelo, for instance. He went on to give some

examples: Handel and Schumann, Balzac and Virginia Woolf,
the poet and hymn writer William Cowper:

> Sometimes a light surprises
> The Christian while he sings:
> It is the Lord who rises
> With healing on his wings;
> When comforts are declining,
> He grants the soul again
> A season of clear shining
> To clear it after rain.

It could be, said the consultant psychiatrist, that on balance
manic depressives are useful people to have around, because
what they have they share.

Miss Bridges didn't seem to share very much. Nobody really
knows when she started to come to church, and when people
finally began to be aware of her presence they assumed she'd
been coming for years and they just hadn't noticed her. 'Who's
the little lady behind the pillar?' Fr Stephens asked his wife.
'I don't know, dear. You're the one who should know that.'
June had been coming to St Michael's for several months in
fact. She hadn't introduced herself because she was too shy.
Besides, you didn't introduce yourself in church. She never
had done in hospital. Besides, you came to church to worship
God, not to meet people. It wasn't a social occasion. Far from
it; being 'matey' in church was really most inappropriate. She
always stayed in her pew in the hospital chapel when it came
to the 'Peace be with you' bit, and she had every intention of
doing so here. (Where had that bit come from anyway? It
crept in when they changed the whole service and started
calling God 'you' instead of 'thou'. It certainly wasn't there
before, she could vouch for that, knowing the Prayer Book
Service of Holy Communion off by heart!)

Once her presence had been noted, Fr Stephens and several
of the congregation attempted to make closer contact, but

without success. She was always the same, polite and mono-syllabic – obviously someone who preferred to 'keep herself to herself'. Fr Stephens enquired as to where she lived so that he might call round and visit her. Could he call on Monday afternoon? June said 'Yes, of course' and smiled at him.

When he arrived she was obviously very pleased to see him. 'Oh, it is nice of you to call, Vicar. It's really lovely to have a visitor. Please have a piece of cake, I went out and bought it specially for you.' Her flat was sparsely furnished and scrupulously clean, and she was wearing a summer frock which made her look much younger than her Sunday outfit of navy blue suit and matching hat. Encouraged by the success of the cake she began very gradually to disclose information about herself. She had been in her flat for six months, for four of which she had been coming to St Michael's. Before that, for forty-five years, she had been a patient at the psychiatric hospital in the neighbouring town. She was admitted when she was twenty years old, on the day after her twentieth birthday: 'I used to hear voices, you know.' She had always hoped to get out, but year followed year, one by one her family died, and she settled down and made it her home. Coming out of hospital after so many years was something of a shock. She had never expected this to happen. It was nice to have a place of your own. She paused, and then said again: 'very nice'. The vicar thought she wasn't going to say anything else, and got ready to ask about the hospital, when Miss Bridges said: 'I always kept myself to myself. I wasn't going to get caught up in all that. All the same, there are people you miss. I suppose it's a long time.' She looked Fr Stephens in the eye: 'I never thought I'd get out,' and added 'It's all right, I don't hear voices now. I don't know what all that was about.' Fr Stephens asked what he could do to help her settle down. She said that he was already doing a lot to help. The church was a great source of comfort and support. 'It was the same when I was in hospital. I don't know what I would have done if I couldn't have gone to the chapel. It was a place of calm in a mad, mad world. Oh I was fond of some of them but now and again I had to get away from the ward squabble and be with myself and God. Now life's much quieter, but I still need my place of refuge, when I can be alone with Him. That's why I sit at the back. I'm not lonely. I hope people don't think I'm stand-offish, but I'd rather just watch and be with Him. No, Vicar, you don't need to do anything at all. What would I do without church?'

The fact that Miss Bridges has spent forty-five years in a psychiatric hospital may seem to make her an extraordinary person. However, she neither appears nor feels in any way extraordinary. She certainly doesn't ask to be treated in any special way. She only asks to be left alone, which is her right. Ordinary church ways of looking after people by including them in as many activities as possible will simply drive her away. On the other hand, if Fr Stephens hadn't called on her he would never have discovered the special circumstances of her background, nor realized that, in fact, in her own way and at her own pace she does need friendship. Because she has spent so long in an institution she will need both advice and practical help from time to time. However, if these things are offered in an intrusive way she will certainly reject them. Like the rest of us, Miss Bridges is both ordinary and extra-ordinary. Like everyone else, she has to be treated as both. Here, as everywhere, therapy consists in the exercise of inter-personal skills. The awareness of ordinary human need takes precedence over skill in symptom recognition.

3

Religion and Madness

It took me almost two months – four visits – to discover why Angela wanted to talk to me. She never seemed to get to the point. She approached me after the Family Communion on Sunday and asked if she could come and see me during the week: 'There's something I must discuss with you.' I said yes, of course, and we fixed up a time. I had never seen her before. Angela was in her mid-forties, a pretty woman but obviously feeling anxious about something, with a tense look about her eyes and a way of biting her lower lip. She still looked strained when she arrived on the Wednesday morning, and I took special note of the need to be as gentle as possible. I was gentle, phrasing my questions with great delicacy, particularly when I learned that she had recently left the local psychiatric hospital where she had been receiving treatment for the past five weeks: 'The doctor calls it anxiety depression.' I began to ask her about her symptoms: what was it like to suffer from anxiety depression? She looked so tense I thought it might help her to talk about it. When she'd finished talking about her symptoms I encouraged her to tell me about herself – was she married? Had she any children? Perhaps she'd like to tell me more about herself? I needed to know these things if I was going to be any help.

Angela told me all she could. In fact she told me a great deal more than I could possibly deal with at a single sitting, and I had someone else to see. I showed her to the door, having arranged for her to come again the following week. I felt I had done quite a lot of listening without intruding in any harmful way. All the same, I had to admit that the strained, nervous look was still there. I resolved to try harder next Wednesday. In the meantime, I'd glance through my lecture notes on anxiety depression ...

When Angela arrived I noticed straight away that she was more relaxed. The signs of tension had largely disappeared and she seemed calmer. At the same time she was just as eager to talk, which she did right through this session and the next one, giving me all sorts of information without really telling me anything. This made me even more eager to get to grips with the source of her anxiety; nobody who was not really anxious – anxious in a psychiatrically significant way – would possibly go on talking like that. I had to get to the root of the matter.

Session four began well, from my point of view, with Angela giving me, on my suggestion, a detailed description of the symptomatology of her condition. There was no doubt that she was anxious: it was exact, apart from a few minor details, precisely as my notes had described it. Half an hour after she had arrived Angela asked for another appointment. I was surprised and said, 'You must like coming here.' 'Oh, yes I do,' she said. 'I like you to talk to me.' I pointed out that it was she who was doing most of the talking! She said that she knew this but she knew that when she was finished, when I had heard everything about her, then I would start to talk. Fascinated, I asked her what it was that I would talk about. 'You will tell me about God,' she said.

Some want to hear about God for the sake of love and for the sake of meaning – if there is any difference, that is. Some have ideas about God that add to their confusion, or feelings about him that increase their despair – if these ideas and feelings can really be said to be about God rather than about a home-made substitute. Some have personal memories of things they have been taught and cannot forget, about him, pictures of him founded upon their relationship with men and women claiming to act in his name. Some confuse God and the church. Ministers are familiar with all these states of mind in their congregations and also, perhaps, in themselves. Users of mental health facilities may or may not be more prone to them than other people. Certainly, religiously inclined people who become mentally ill tend to have opinions and ideas that are more extreme than average, both about themselves and other people. When this happens the results are clear enough, even to the psychiatrically uninitiated. They are the results of being ill, not of being religious, although if a person thinks in a religious way, if religious ideas play a key part in the way he or she makes sense of life, psychiatric illnesses are likely to express themselves in religious language simply because they are illnesses of thinking and feeling. This is not to say that religious factors play no part in actually causing mental illness. Some people believe that there is a sense in which this kind of illness is actually learned, and that the sense of worthlessness symptomatic of depression refers to the guilt associated with some kinds of religious teaching. Similarly, the confusion about personal relationships which bedevils schizophrenia has been associated with the unacknowledged gap between 'spiritual' perfection and 'actual' behaviour. The fact that emotionally significant people who say they are holy act in ways that obviously are not so may discredit them, or it may deprive holiness itself of its usefulness as a way of making sense of life. On the other hand, this kind of unacknowledged contradiction may dull the edge of all kinds of contradiction, making it easier for opposites to merge and important distinctions to grow hazy. The result of this might be that a reduced or weakened idea of holiness, one which was no longer really different from anything else, might assert itself everywhere in a person's mind. Because religion was no longer special, no longer different from anything else, everything one thought about was religious.

I must say that some of the people I have known who have been accused of having 'religious mania' have been like this, their abnormality consisting in a tendency to 'drag religion

into everything', which stood in sharp contrast to most
people's way of setting it firmly on one side. Religious maniacs
are people who live in a state of perpetual excitement about
religion, however unsuitable or inappropriate such a reaction
might be – when for example they have suffered a severe
personal blow and might be expected to be feeling at least
subdued, if not actually confounded. Behaviour of this kind
is certainly abnormal; although here again it does not stand
out so clearly in communities held together by religious faith
as it does in ordinary twentieth-century Western circles. On
the whole I don't think it is a useful category for ministers to
use. When it crops up it is unmistakable and – like all mania –
very difficult to deal with. You will be able to tell from the
sheer intensity and unremitting nature of the excitement that
psychiatric help is needed. Whether or not you will be able to
convince the person involved is a different matter. If you and
your congregation manage to contain a situation until the
mania lessens (manias usually come in phases), you will have
triumphed in a way that no hospital could. All the same, you
will need the advice and help of a psychiatrist. Actually,
containment is precisely what is needed. Actual psychiatric
treatment is often very much hampered by the fact that maniac
patients are hard to convince of the necessity to take their
tablets. Why should they, if they aren't ill? They go on being
'high' until their mania burns itself out. To be members of a
congregation that understands and cares is by far the best
thing for them, and can have a calming effect which is much
more significant for their lives than medication (particularly
medication you don't actually get round to taking!).

In contrast to this, the tendency to supply complicated
religious reasons for what can be perfectly straightforward
events belongs to thinking rather than feeling, the type of
thinking associated with the schizoid determination to have
everything make the same kind of sense. Because religion is
the most important thing it becomes the only important thing.
This, however, is a matter of abnormal thought rather than

excessive feeling. People who think like this are not harmed by attending worship. There is no evidence that their 'symptoms' become more pronounced. I suspect that they make up a very valuable section of a typical congregation. Although people of both these kinds will probably have spent some time in a psychiatric hospital, they don't regard themselves as mad in any far-reaching way. Indeed, from a religious point of view they are not. I certainly believe that we should not be too quick to discount their saneness.

It should always be remembered that seeing life in ways sometimes associated with mental illness is not the same thing as actually being mentally ill. People live with their symptoms more or less under control for long periods of their life. Sometimes their symptoms are controlled by tablets, sometimes by injections administered at intervals of a month or so. Often their illness is in abeyance, and their symptoms are much less disturbing to themselves and other people. Often, of course, they are actually better, in which case their 'illness' is simply the stigma that still attaches to them, which is just as hard to treat if not harder.

The particular clusters of ways of experience and reacting to life that we are used to calling mental illnesses relate closely to the kinds of personality type that develops them. Schizophrenia, for instance, is associated with thinking-type people, those who could be expected to think their way through feelings rather than react emotionally to events, as people do who are prone to depression. This certainly does not mean that deep-thinking people are prone to schizophrenia, or that the tender hearted are likely to become clinically depressed. The association is not a causal one: it was arrived at retrospectively by noticing that people with these psychiatric diagnoses tended to be these kinds of personalities. That is, they exhibited these personality traits in their normal 'pre-morbid' lives, and returned to them when crises of illness had passed. From this point of view mental illness can be understood as a personality characteristic that has got out of hand and temporarily taken control of the personality.

The implications of this for the church are tremendous. Somehow we must stop treating ex-patients as dangerous aliens and start valuing them for the very positive gifts of personality and character that they undoubtedly possess. They are people that we need among us – deep-thinking, imaginative people; emphatic, tender-hearted people, people anxious to belong and to contribute; people who think differently and provide new insights into old situations. Here is something that we can do better than our fathers and mothers did. By taking the emotionally wounded into our congregations we gain an immense new resource for the church. In so doing we fulfil the law of Christ, which is the law of mutual love, the interchange of caring. We need each other.

Certainly we need them; but they need us more. Ours is a lost opportunity, a neglected resource. Theirs is the continuing experience of loneliness and rejection: the feeling that nobody cares which affects so many psychiatric 'users'. Now that it is almost impossible to obtain residential psychiatric accommodation for anybody who is not in the acute phase of illness, many who would formerly have been taken into hospital live in bedsitters and hostels. Whatever may be said of the older psychiatric hospitals, at their best they functioned like small towns or large villages. There were people to talk to and places to go. Long-term friendships and lively antagonisms flourished there. Quite often people didn't want to leave, a condition usually described as institutionalization, but often more like common sense; the house was empty, the husband or wife had died, the neighbours had moved. There was nothing there.

What people who have been ill need is friendship. As Christians we should not need to have to remind ourselves of this. We are required to take part, along with the rest of society, in an intensive social revolution that involves integrating the mentally ill into the community. Compared with many social revolutions this may seem insignificant. It isn't. The old county mental hospitals of the early nineteenth century represent a systematic attempt to control the problem of mental disturbance by removing mentally ill people from society as a whole and creating a special place for them 'outside the camp'. (It is amazing how many of the early hospitals were built in precisely that situation, just a few miles from the town or city centre. Later hospitals were moved further away, into the middle of the countryside.) Having contained the problem in this way, it was obviously important to make sure that contact with the neighbouring communities would be kept to a minimum. Once made, the breach must be maintained in the face of normal human curiosity and friendliness. As the years went by, the hospitals came to symbolize everything that was forbidden, despised and rejected, on the principle of the taboo imputed to things specially set apart that renders them unclean. It had to be so in order to maintain the marginalization of the mentally ill designed to protect society as a whole from people who could not, or would not, fit and yet might not legitimately be punished for it.

At the beginning of the twenty-first century we have got to do better than this. The amount of ingenuity, time and resources devoted by nineteenth-century administrators to marginalizing the mentally ill has not been mirrored in the present government's efforts at returning them to the community. In some places very little has been done. Hospitals have been closed down before alternative accommodation has been provided. Individual patients have been moved into flats and hostels. Some have left the neighbourhood, the hospital doesn't know where. In most areas there are drop-in centres like the one mentioned earlier, or day centres provided by the local authority. There are very few such places, however, and there were thousands of patients. Generally speaking, the general public is not aware of the significance of this bungled piece of social engineering which seeks to demolish one century's solution to the problem of human mental breakdown without supplying another.

This, in short, is the situation which the church faces, simply by being part of the community. Some see it as a tremendous challenge, some as an attempt on the government's part to unload its own responsibilities on to others. I have heard church people ask why the church's slender resources should be spent in looking after people for whom it is the state's duty to provide. At least they showed some understanding of the size of the task. Most people in the church, however, seem unaware of what is really happening. They are not aware of the tremendous implications of such a move on the part of the state, a move that puts them and their fellow Christians in the front line of caring for a socially stigmatized minority. Unfortunately for those who would have it otherwise, those in authority within the National Health Service see the churches as their natural allies in the process of communitization. The local congregation, they say, is the obvious place for ex-patients to find friendship and support. The church claims to welcome people: here are people in need of a welcome. If the church considers this attitude to represent a kind of blackmail, so much the pity. It doesn't reflect very well on the church. The job is there, it is their kind of job, how can they refuse?

There is no doubt that this is the government's expectation. The NHS and Community Care Act of 1990 stated that services should be provided that allow 'people who are affected by the problems of ageing, mental illness, mental handicap or physical sensory disability to be able to live as independently as possible in their own homes, or in homely settings within the community'. Few people would disagree that life 'within the community' is likely to be preferable to life within an institution set apart from the rest of the world (as well as being cheaper for the authorities, of course!). The official policy of regarding an ideal as a fait accompli, however, has presented local authorities with a task that they cannot hope to carry out unassisted. All over the country the church is being encouraged to become part of the 'interdisciplinary team' providing care within the community.

To be fair to the church, the challenge has not been ignored. In a recent paper from the Board of Social Responsibility of the Anglican General Synod, the Bishop of Liverpool, David Sheppard, drew attention to the major role the church has to play in pastoral care for all individuals in the community: 'Above all, it needs to discover that those with mental illness have gifts and abilities which can enrich the whole community.' He went on to draw attention to the real difficulty in the way of putting these to work: 'There is still a real stigma surrounding mental illness which will not be eradicated by exhortation and rhetoric.' Some congregations have worked hard to overcome this stigma. In many parts of Great Britain individual churches and groups of congregations have opened drop-in centres or set up counselling and support services or friendship clubs. Because it is rare to find neighbouring congregations of the same denomination which share this interest, most of these initiatives are ecumenical ventures. Even so, they are still very thin on the ground. For instance, a town which had a large mental hospital now has several user support groups; the neighbouring town, with a mental hospital as big, has none at all.

A vital means of support for ex-patients is the Association for the Pastoral Care of the Mentally Ill, an ecumenical organization seeking to enable Christians to undertake this kind of work. The Association points out that there are various ways in which individual Christians and churches can be supportive. Firstly, simply by being with people, supporting, listening, being a friend. Secondly, giving practical help where needed. The third way is to provide an environment in which people can meet one another and increase their circle of friends. The fourth lies in the area of educating the Christian community and making it more aware of the situation which exists and its implications for them as Christians. This can range from trying to remove the fear of mental illness by holding seminars and giving lectures, to helping churches to reach their potential for being an essential part of the caring process within the community so that they can influence the decisions made by the authorities in their mental health strategy for the region, city or neighbourhood. Membership is individual or group – and, of course, donations are very much appreciated!

The work done by churches in simply making users and ex-users welcome at services and social events cannot be underestimated. As an ex-patient said to me, 'People don't want their whole lives dominated by "mental health activities". It's nice to have places of our own to go to; but we want to be able to go other places as well.' Going to church is just as important as going to the drop-in centre run by MIND or the local authority day centre for psychiatric service users. Much as these initiatives are appreciated for the company they provide, they have the disadvantage of reminding ex-patients of a side of life that they would prefer to forget. Although it may sometimes be a case of 'any port in a storm', ex-patients do not always want to attend a day centre designed specially for them. They would rather choose their own friends and find their own haunts. Even though they feel self-conscious in case people find out, they would much rather run the risk of exposure as someone from 'that place' than let society choose their friends for them. After all, they are better now; why go on being a special case? This is a common reaction to the provision of special facilities for ex-patients. However attractive and well run they may be, they have the disadvantage of perpetuating the old division, the one they exist to remove. Ex-patients are housed on the same council estate, go to the same pubs and cafés, meet at the same social centre. They form a group for mutual protection, a kind of psychiatric ghetto. The new system begins to resemble the old one. The only way round this is that of personal befriending, by which individuals are drawn together by interest and attraction rather than thrown together because they belong to the same social groupings. Of all social institutions the churches are in the best position to do this, as they contain all kinds of people, of every background and interest, drawn together to serve the ideal of love.

4

Mainly About Handicap

Jenny and Margaret live with two other women at Lea House, a psychiatric group home situated at the other end of the parish. They have been living there for five years. Before that they were residents of a new hospital for mental handicap situated fifteen miles away, where they had lived most of their lives. Margaret and Jenny are the only ones who go to church. One of the reasons why they chose to live in the same group home was that they are both Roman Catholics and felt that this made them belong together. They love coming to Holy Name and never miss a Sunday, except when they are on holiday. They turn up when one, or both, is really too poorly to come. Last Sunday, for instance, Margaret was obviously just starting flu and had to be sent back home in case she gave it to the children. When this was pointed out she went back home without any fuss. The children are 'the most important thing, aren't they?'.

When they first came to Holy Name five years ago, two young women of twenty-eight and thirty, it was the children that caught their eye. Jenny, the older and more confident, went straight over and sat next to them, staying with them for the whole service. 'Why didn't you come?' she asked Margaret, who grinned and didn't say anything. Next week she went across as well, and every other week. Someone said to the parish priest, 'Those two young women are very good with the children.' He said that he was very glad to hear it, perhaps they'd like to help with them on an official basis. When it was pointed out to him that they were mentally handicapped he said, 'Does that matter?'

As it turned out, it hasn't done. When they don't know what to do, they ask. The kids obviously see them as friends, possibly elder sisters, never as parent substitutes. Their experience of life in a large institution has made them aware of the need to keep rules so that, if anything, both of them tend to err on the conformist side. Over against this, however, is their spontaneous sense of fun. They see the opportunity for a laugh even before the children do, and usually take it, deflecting the wrath of the parents on to themselves and so winning the undying devotion of the kids. In fact Jenny and Margaret do a remarkable job in bridging the generation gap between adults and children. Perhaps being somehow in the middle between adult and child they identify with both sides. Instead of standing out as strangers in the congregation because of their handicap, they play an important role in its corporate identity, holding it together as a family. Their uninhibited friendliness is particularly appreciated by those isolated by suffering: 'She came over and smiled and sat by me. I think that people were feeling embarrassed, you see, and didn't want to upset me. They didn't know what to say, but she just came over and smiled.' Certainly, any congregation can use that sort of thing. 'These two women they live with, are they Catholics too?' said the parish priest hopefully.

It seems to be much easier for mentally handicapped people – or people with 'learning difficulties' as they are called nowadays – to gain acceptance in ordinary social groups than it is for mentally ill people or those known to have been suffering from mental illness. The fear that attracts itself to mental illness – of the unknown and the unpredictable, the highly-developed myth of lunacy which has been part of Western culture for so many generations – has as its object much more than what used to be called 'simple-mindedness'. Mentally handicapped people have found themselves excluded from society as a result of their inability to conform, which means competing with others on the same terms. They have been provided with special sheltered environments and patronized as not fully human because of their disablement. By turns neglected and patronized, they have rarely been feared – except by those who fear difference of any kind at all.

Mental illness can be very frightening because everyone, including the suffering person themselves, has a sense of not quite knowing what is going on. We shall see that this seems to be a basic characteristic of the whole group of illnesses known as psychoses, which are characterized among other things by a mis-match of worlds, in which individuals experience their own 'inner' world as seriously out of line with the 'outer' world of other people. In order to maintain itself in the face of the world of common sense this private view indulges in all sorts of stratagems aimed at baffling the opposition or making converts. The result is a general sense of unreality in which nobody, even the sick person themselves, can be quite certain what is going on – a frightening situation, and one which brings home to us the degree to which our relationships depend on the assumption of a common frame of reference. The implication here is that someone is not simply holding something back, but that they are living in a different kind of world.

Mentally handicapped people are certainly in our world, however. Anyone less sinister than a mentally handicapped person would be hard to imagine. Generally speaking, they signal their feelings and intentions – including the intention to deceive – rather more clearly than most people do. If they are frightening, it is more likely to be because of the lack of ability to control violent emotions than the suggestion of a hidden threat of any kind. Unless they are unfortunate enough to suffer from some kind of mental illness, the mentally handicapped are usually very straightforward indeed. Refreshingly so. There is a whole world of difference between mental illness and mental handicap and they should never be confused.

Mentally handicapped people have suffered from the assumption that the two conditions are similar. After all, they both centre upon the mind and involve doctors. If mentally ill people are incarcerated, then surely mentally handicapped people should be too. In a sense, however, the mentally ill are already incarcerated, already alienated by their condition. To give them a special place to be, so that they can work through their isolation before emerging again into the world, makes a kind of sense for the mentally ill. For the mentally handicapped it makes no sense at all.

Perhaps I ought to say at this point that I am not writing about mental illness and mental handicap as such, but about my own experiences and impressions. My treatment of these important subjects is impressionistic rather than systematic; but there are many books that can be consulted, some more approachable than others.

Impressionistic or not, there are certain basic facts that stand out clearly, and must be grasped first of all. The first of these is the difference between mental illness and mental handicap. Mentally handicapped people suffer from the results of brain damage sustained at birth or in the womb, or from an inherited genetic imbalance. As a result they do not develop in the way, or to the extent, that other people do. Their personalities are child- or adolescent-like. This can be misleading for strangers, who expect them to 'behave the age that they look'. They cannot be considered 'ill' in the same way that mentally ill people are. Within these limitations they live ordinary lives and form ordinary relationships. The fact that the two things, mental illness and mental handicap, are thought of together shows the confusion that exists on the part of the public when such things are talked about.

(It seems that everybody – including a mentally handicapped person – can become mentally *ill*. Mental illness is something you develop and from which you recover; which is why it is called an illness or group of illnesses. Actually it isn't as simple as that; most psychiatrists agree that those who become ill have a 'predisposition' towards illness, some kind of genetic tendency towards a particular kind of mental breakdown; the breakdown passes but the underlying tendency remains, and probably recurs. A minority of psychiatrists – and the majority of clinical psychologists – appear to favour an interpretation of mental illness in terms of 'learned behaviour': certain ways of relating to other people – actually, of *avoiding* relating to them – are learned early in life as a way of defending oneself from the emotional pain involved in trying to make relationships in situations of extreme emotional confusion. This approach necessitates a process of emotional re-learning and depends for this on the quality of relationship between patient and therapist and the latter's skill in helping the former untie his or her psychological knots. The first group of psychiatrists depend more upon relieving distress by removing the most painful symptoms of illness: the roots of the condition cannot really be reached because they are literally built into the system. This is by far the larger and more influential group. Apart from anything else it produces quicker results and consequently recommends itself to the NHS – and, of course, to private medicine as well.)

There are several kinds of mental handicap, but they all involve a reduction in intellectual ability and a limitation in emotional scope and flexibility, though not necessarily in intensity. As we shall see, this isn't the case with mental illness. This does not usually affect intelligence (for example we have the stereotype of the 'mad scientist'). It does, however, alter a person's grasp of reality. Different illnesses affect one's view of oneself, of other people, of particular events and environments, causing one to react in ways that appear to other people to be inappropriate and self-destructive, even when protection rather than destruction is the objective. The symptoms of mental illness can be so terrifying to the person suffering them that he or she searches for ways of bringing them to an end that seem 'mad' to other people – by inventing alternative worlds and universes to live in, or by committing suicide, to make sure that this one has no power to inflict further torment. Our ministry is to try to relieve this distress. We will work as ministers normally work: by holding services and preaching, by 'pastoral conversations' in which men and women seek for verbal assurances of God's personal love towards them and talk in confidence about the things that trouble them; by the Sacrament of Forgiveness if this forms a part of their professional custom: and if it does not, then an equally authoritative and definite way of getting the message across; by being available to listen and talk, not always busy doing something else; by regularly visiting the places where people live, their wards, homes, hostels.

If ministry to mentally ill people is basically the same as ministry to anybody in distress, ministry to people with 'learning difficulties' is more straightforward still. It's a pity to regard mental handicap as a pastoral problem. Generally speaking, if there's a problem it's with us, not them. Not that this is entirely our fault. For generations, mentally handicapped and mentally ill people have been bracketed together, by the arrangements made by society to look after them. Sometimes they have lived together as co-inmates of the same huge asylum, so that it eventually becomes impossible to tell the difference between them, and mentally handicapped men and women were treated as though they were ill, receiving the same crude psychiatric medication as the other inmates. Together or apart, both groups of people, being shut away, shared the same stigma.

This is the situation that we have all inherited and there is no doubt who the losers are. People who should have been able to enjoy a normal life in an ordinary family have been treated in a special way and encouraged to play the role of patients – to become patients with the strict regulation of personal behaviour, the inhibition of mutuality and limitation of personal freedom that such a role involves when it is played full-time over many years. Nowadays we know very well that this is quite an inappropriate treatment for anyone at all, never mind for those who have so much to contribute to community, and yet the mere fact of abnormality, plus the crippling association with actual mental illness, is enough to isolate the handicapped within the community they have at last been allowed to rejoin. Some mentally handicapped people have medical syndromes which may or may not make them look slightly different from other people (Down's Syndrome is a good example). I don't think, from the mentally handicapped people I have known, that they are particularly conscious of being any different from anyone else. They tend to see themselves in a very factual way, as simply themselves. They don't make comparisons, except among themselves. It's we who make comparisons.

Unfortunately we don't make them very well. We don't make them in accordance with the facts. People with learning difficulties who are living in ordinary neighbourhoods find ways of contributing to the life of the neighbourhood – doing shopping for the elderly housebound, baby-sitting and looking after small children, gardening and doing various manual jobs – anything, in fact, that a particular individual may be able to do. Mental handicap may affect a person's intelligence without affecting other mental abilities. Some are particularly sensitive and intuitive; many are artistic. The more direct and expressive world of plays, where situations are shown forth with the kind of clarity rarely achieved in life, allow them a kind of release from the frustration of ordinary self-expression. Any parish with both a group home or hostel for people with learning difficulties *and a dramatic society* is in a fortunate position!

Everybody is different and this certainly applies to a category as broad as 'learning difficulties'. People described like this can be interested in, drawn to, capable of, even good at, a whole range of activities and subjects which bring them into contact with others and contribute a very great deal to the life of the community. Their disability may affect the way they speak or walk, but the chance is that they are not very conscious of such things, having 'always been like this'. Some handicapped people tend to be easily upset if they can't get their own way; a characteristic which seems to relate to the childish or child-like personality which so many, if not all of them have. These upsets are soon forgotten, however, as they are with children; it is almost unthinkable to involve the mentally handicapped in the kind of long-term mis-understandings that 'normal' people enjoy, and that cause misery within congregations. The presence of these men and women in any group of worshippers can be a great asset so far as spontaneity and whole-heartedness are concerned; again, there is a child-like excitement at joining in. The com-munion services at the Mental Handicap Hospital where I worked for many years as a member of the chaplaincy team were the liveliest I have ever come across, with all sorts of alarms and excursions, all sorts of interruptions. And yet they possessed a quality of truth, a kind of simple seriousness that I have never come across anywhere else. When people question the ability of the mentally handicapped to 'under-stand about God' I remember these communions ... I shall never forget them.

Certainly, not all those with learning difficulties are like this – enthusiastic, quarrelsome, spontaneous and affec-tionate. Like the rest of us, they have 'off times' when their handicap renders them harder to reach, more different than they are. Talking about them I have to admit that I am at something of a disadvantage despite the fact that I have known so many of them. To me they are simply people. I never learned how to put them into psychiatric categories. Perhaps I was fortunate not to. I liked and disliked them as themselves, people I knew. Obviously, as I got to know a particular person I would become aware of his or her strengths and weaknesses, the way one does without making any great effort to do so. Mentally handicapped people make this par-ticularly easy by taking the initiative in getting to know you and keeping the relationship going in case you might somehow forget them. Enthusiasm is their strong point, and they will often rush at whatever it is they have to do without taking the trouble to consider its difficulties and problems beforehand. Consequently they are liable to undertake tasks which are quite beyond their abilities out of the sheer joy of self-expression and in the desire to please. Most clergy find this irresistible, of course. They only wish that such a spirit of co-operation was more widespread. Are they confirmed? Would they like to be? And almost always they would. They aren't all enthusiastic, quarrelsome and affectionate, of course. This is simply the over-riding impression I have gained in eighteen years' experience.

Should they be confirmed? Of course they should! Learning difficulties don't stop a person believing in God, although their belief seems simple and childish compared with the vicar's. The awareness of the holy is well-developed in people who find difficulty in describing what it is exactly that they feel, apart from saying things like 'I feel God'. Certainly there are some practical difficulties, but these concern worship rather than theology. The mentally handicapped have no difficulty at all with the Trinity, but are likely to guffaw loudly when something funny attracts their attention during the service. People who should have known better have claimed that absence of intellect necessarily involves absence of soul; theologians have asked how people with learning difficulties of a genetic kind could possibly be made 'in the image of God'. In other words, they have assumed that God's perfection is intellectual, and our main link with him is by means of our ability to understand things about him. The argument goes so far as to urge that all chaplains to mental handicap hospitals should henceforth consider themselves to be redundant and return to their parishes because they are simply wasting their time. Ideas like these are particularly abhorrent to anybody who has been fortunate enough to serve as pastor to mentally handicapped people. Identifying mind and soul is a hoary old blasphemy and would normally be ignored; it is within the context of actual experience – the reality of fellowship expressed in common worship, a marvellous shared awareness of God – that ideas like this are exposed in all their crassness.

Take Albert, for instance.

Albert was the mainstay of the Tuesday afternoon communion service. He had been coming to church since he was a small child, living in a succession of homes for the mentally subnormal, and had always taken an important part in the service. When I was leading the service Albert would assume the office of clerk, keeping order in the congregation, bringing in the collection plate and serving for the communion. He was always smartly turned out, usually in a suit, with his father's silver watch and chain. (At some point during the previous years one of the local vicars had enlisted Albert into the Church of England Men's Society and he was always urging me to set up a branch within the hospital. 'Come on, Mr Grainger. We could meet on Friday nights.' Whether the idea would have been feasible, I don't know; unfortunately the CEMS ceased to be shortly afterwards so I never found out.) When the hospital began to move its residents into the community and Albert went to live in a group home he joined the congregation of St Philip's. I don't think anybody knew where he came from. After a while they became used to his presence in church on a Sunday, always bright and friendly, never saying much but always looking well turned-out. Gradually, people began to talk to him. They found themselves getting to know someone surprising, someone totally different from anyone they had ever met before.

Albert has that rare gift, a totally instinctive sense of humour. The things he says are funny and – what is much rarer – he makes the things you say seem funny, too. The expression on his face is that of someone just about to break into laughter. For the time being, however, he is simply smiling, which is his usual expression. A church with Albert in its congregation is perpetually on the brink of mirth. Not that he ever actually laughs during the service; as a sidesperson it is part of his job to make sure that improper conduct is discouraged, and he carries out his job with total devotion. Albert likes things to be done properly, quietly, and in order. He carefully chose St Philip's for its Anglican 'sobriety', having first tried out the more charismatic versions of church-manship. The arrangement works extremely well; St Philip's keeps up the tradition of the church Albert knew best, to which he was taken every Sunday during his years at the hospital.

Last year Albert was absent from church on three successive Sundays. Eventually, wondering what had happened, one of the other sidespersons, Victor, called round to the group home where he lived. Perhaps he was ill and needed help? It turned out that Albert had flu. The people he shared the house with had already been in touch with the Community Psychiatric Nurse and she had called round a few days earlier. Albert was sitting up in bed, with a mug of hot milk in his hand. He looked very sorry for himself but he was obviously being looked after very well.

Next week Albert was back in church, beaming at every-body as usual. The visit had been a useful one. Besides making contact with the other residents of the group home, Victor had taken the trouble to enquire about the nurse who had visited Albert. How would one contact her if the need should ever arise? The vicar rang the number Victor had been given and spoke to the nurse herself, telling her of his – and the parish's – connection with Albert. He seized the opportunity to invite her to come along and talk about her work to the next church meeting. 'Most people have no idea of what a Community Psychiatric Nurse is,' he said. The nurse said that she would be delighted to come and talk – not many people seemed interested enough to ask her. Quite a few turned up out of solidarity with Albert and heard about the nurse's daily routine of visiting former patients of the mental illness and mental handicap hospitals and her work with new patients referred by the GP.

One of the things that the vicar – and various members of the congregation – learned from the episode was how pleasant it is to visit a group home. As Fr Stephens discovered when he called on Miss Bridges, the role of host is a grateful one for those who have spent years of their lives in premises not their own. People who live in group homes ask very little of the community to which they have been returned, simply a smile and a nod. They don't expect to be visited; after all, they don't really feel they belong. One of them told me that she still didn't feel that she really belonged in the large residential estate where she had been living for the last ten years. She remembered the farm where she spent her childhood and, of course, the hospital. These were real places: 'I feel I'm a visitor here.' Which is why people who live in group homes enjoy having visitors so much. They don't only enjoy having visitors, they *must* have them if they are ever going to settle down properly and become part of the community. The process is reciprocal. Of course, we have to get used to having them drop in on us – and to being as hospitable as they are!

As a local clergyman or a member of a church congregation, you are very likely to meet men and women with learning difficulties. You will want to make them as welcome as possible. Very likely they will have been to church before, as many handicap hospitals are in the habit of running car loads of their residents to local churches each Sunday – a very good arrangement indeed as far as the residents are concerned, as people with learning difficulties nearly always appreciate an outing, particularly if it involves a good sing. Their obvious enjoyment of church soon wins friends in the congregation who look forward to their visits to church as much as they do.

Now they will be members of the congregation in a way that they could never be before, when they all came over together in one party from the hospital and sat in the front pews. Now you will have to get to know them as individuals, and to do so without any specific guidelines, only a very general understanding that this person has lived a socially restricted life and looks at the world through eyes that are a good deal younger than her or his age. People with learning difficulties can have any of the personality and character tendencies that other members of the congregation have. Each individual must be met as an individual – a person, not a case. This is true even if, as may well happen, he or she is unfortunate enough to have a mental illness as well as difficulty in learning. Certainly, nobody deserves to be treated as if their difficulty *were* itself an illness.

Increased community care has brought a group of people out of hospital who really are ill, and usually old as well. These are people suffering from progressive degenerative disorders of the brain, including Alzheimer's disease, who are now being cared for in local homes for the elderly. Strictly speaking, they should not be included in a chapter on learning difficulties, because their condition does not originate at birth but arrives much later. I don't need to describe the pathetic state of these poor people except to say that they seem to have been stripped of all human dignity by the illness. No one can really be sure whether they have any real awareness of what is happening to them, and their loved ones are distressed because someone who knew them intimately seems to have forgotten who they are. Instinctively, they go on talking as if deep down they are making some kind of contact. Perhaps we should do the same.

MENCAP, the Royal Society for Mentally Handicapped Children and Adults, is probably the most 'user-friendly' of all the societies which aim at helping people with psychiatric difficulties. It has a great number of local branches, which, generally speaking, are well supported by the public. Thanks to the hard work put in by MENCAP, people with learning difficulties are thought of, and treated, in an entirely different way nowadays. Gone is the attitude of mind that once regarded them as 'better kept out of sight'. Now they enjoy the same rights and opportunities as the rest of us, and often make just as good use of them – if not better!

5

Mental Illness

Sylvia was a member of my confirmation class. She is one of those people who appear to have discovered the secret of eternal youth. She was around forty at the time, and looked at least twenty-five. I had known her for several years when she asked to be confirmed. Her mother was a regular church-goer and it was almost certainly she who had suggested the idea to Sylvia. I can't say that I was looking forward to the confirmation classes, because Sylvia has difficulty in concentrating on anything for very long. I didn't know her as well as I would have liked to because conversation was always hard to sustain. It was as if her mind was dancing around all over the place so that you couldn't keep up with her for more than a couple of seconds at a time; once you thought she had started to take notice of what you were saying she would say something on a completely different tack, and you realized she was off somewhere chasing a butterfly of her own. I suppose I should have tried to follow her, to see what she was seeing, but I imagined my job to be that of an instructor, someone concerned with getting information across – and with Sylvia this was very difficult.

On the other hand Sylvia was willing to take the will for the deed. She knew I was trying hard, and, whenever she thought I might be on the point of giving up and calling it a day, she would say, 'There, there. It doesn't matter.' (On one occasion I had to apologize to her for forgetting to bring a cross and chain I had promised her. She threw her arms around my neck and kissed me – 'It doesn't matter, Mr Grainger, love, don't you worry about it.') When it became obvious that our leisurely pace was holding the others back I arranged to see Sylvia privately; the ceremony was getting nearer, and I really felt she ought to know something about the rudiments of the faith: it was, after all, my responsibility. It didn't get any easier. In fact it was harder under the new system, harder to keep hold of Sylvia's concentration, harder to avoid the temptation to relax and simply have a chat. Why couldn't we talk about the new carpet? It wasn't that she was uninterested in Moses and Jesus. Just that she was interested in so much else as well.

Obviously I was expecting her to be able to cope with ideas quite beyond her grasp. I could find out by asking what had I just been saying? Could she remember? Surprisingly she always could. She knew just what I had been saying. She even knew what I was going to ask next. I felt rather annoyed at the thought that she had been there before me all the time and accused her of playing me along – 'All this I've been telling you, you know it already, don't you?' Very patiently and with great kindness, as if she were talking to a small child, Sylvia said, 'Well, love, I've been a Christian for a long time, haven't I?'

Sylvia was diagnosed as schizophrenic. Not all schizophrenics are as happy as that, however. All the same, I have noticed some things about them that they do appear to have in common, ways of behaving which I have noticed a tendency towards in almost everybody I have met who, at one time or another, has received the diagnosis. This is not really surprising, however, because mental illnesses are ways of describing collections of signs and symptoms that tend to occur together, rather than recognizable diseases in which it is possible to determine how, when and why something has gone wrong with the way the human organism works. I must say again, however, that my conclusions are not medical ones. If you are interested to learn the 'official' judgments about mental illness you would be advised to consult one of the authorities mentioned in the bibliography at the end of this book. My own background and training are more psychological and theological than psychiatric, as will appear in the following notes.

Schizophrenia is generally accepted to be a condition affecting thought, affecting the emotions at second hand, via ideation. It is a 'disorder of cognition'. Generally speaking it is characterized by an immense amount of thinking with very few conclusions. Because there are so few firm conclusions reached, thinking becomes an endless task – or rather it would do if it had to obey the rules of normal interpersonal communication, which is goal-oriented and must achieve a certain kind of shape. Schizophrenic people appear to be overpowered by the sheer pressure of thoughts which, because they are not properly organized, never allow time for pauses, the natural moment of relaxation we enjoy when we have 'made our point', 'reached a conclusion'. One thing leads to another, and another until it has all been included. This is impossible, of course. To avoid the extreme distress caused by perpetual failure, the practical usefulness of thought as a way of communicating real ideas to others and oneself gives way to thought as a distraction, a fascinating game which doesn't in the long run really mean anything at all . . .

People who show signs of schizophrenic thought disorder have difficulty in making meaningful distinctions between things, so that they cannot efficiently assess the relative importance of the things that happen to them, particularly when they involve other people. One way of putting this is to say that they lack the ability to characterize – to know what to expect of other people, and consequently how to change their behaviour in accordance with changes in the inter-personal situation. Characterization depends on the ability to distinguish 'this' from 'that'; if you have no efficient system for characterizing people and things you live in a fluid indeterminate world in which nothing is unthinkable and hardly anything recognizable. A schizophrenic person may confuse the idea of being 'in Christ' with that of actually being Christ because they appear to him or her to be the same idea, with nothing to choose between them, no meaningful distinction. For us they are two separate propositions, the first thinkable, the second literally and metaphorically unthinkable. This kind of consideration does not stop a schizophrenic person from confusing the two statements, however. In schizophrenic thought nothing is less thinkable than anything else. Metaphor, poetic reality which runs alongside the ordinary world and comments upon it, is beyond the reach of this kind of awareness. Psychiatrists draw attention to the symptom of 'concrete thinking' which takes things in the most literal way and consistently misunderstands figures of speech. Similarly, people whose thinking is disordered in this way regard words and phrases which have two or more meanings as if the distinction was semantically unimportant, slipping from one meaning to another without acknowledging any distinction, simply enjoying the extra space provided by the link. (For example, a patient told me that 'we had strawberries and cream for tea, so I hope these tablets work better than the last did'. It turned out that he was making a connection between 'treatment' and 'a treat'. This was not pointed out at the time, however. It resulted in what psychologists call 'the knight's move', in which the logic of somebody's communication involves vital stages which are left unspecified, so that the argument seems to have moved, as in chess, 'two steps forward and one to the left' instead of 'three steps forward', thus confusing the listener.)

These things are touched upon here because they are relevant to any job which involves communicating with people suffering from any degree of schizophrenic thought disorder. The question as to how the condition originated does not directly concern us here. As a personal opinion, I would favour an explanation which takes account of the effects of early experience rather than one depending on the presence of a genetic imbalance. Certainly, patients with thought disorder commonly have abnormal patterns of electrical activity in their brains; but many people who are not afflicted in this way have similar brain waves. More significantly, there seems to be a definite link between the signs and symptoms of thought disorder and the kinds of environment from which patients came. The argument, briefly, is that children learn to avoid making meaningful distinctions because they have been presented with a confusing model of behaviour and attitude – one in which whatever they choose to do and think turns out to be wrong, and every lesson learned is systematically negated, usually at the same time and by the same people. The connection between this kind of experience and opting out of drawing conclusions is obvious. Life in a world where nothing ever turns out the way you expect and you can't ever be sure how anything you say or do will be received by the key figures in your life may well contribute to a state of mind in which you learn to 'hedge your bets', refusing to let yourself make important distinctions between what is valuable and worthless, important and trivial, exciting and dull, tragic and comic, etc. When your assessments of value, importance, excitement, tragedy, have been shown to be wide of the mark as often as they have been validated by other people, you cease to pay all that much attention to what other people say or do – after all, you simply never know what to expect, and even *they* don't seem to be able to make up their minds.

There are many ways in which this kind of confusion can occur in someone's life. The blame does not always have to be laid at the door of the parents. In the same way, there should be ways of working towards unravelling it. The eminent Personal Construct Psychologist, Don Bannister, worked long and hard in the effort to encourage thought-disordered patients to trust their own conclusions, so that they could invest meaning in them and learn again to attribute different degrees of personal significance to people and things, thus distinguishing among them. I have carried out research in this area myself, and am convinced that this kind of thought disorder can to a large extent be reversed if you can find a way of taking the communication of schizophrenic people seriously and bringing home to them the fact that you take what they are saying as a valid communication of a valid meaning.

Thought-disordered people tend to talk a lot, in the eager but not very hopeful attempt to get across to their usually not very attentive listeners. Depressed people are, of course, totally different. Here you will find that you are the one who has difficulty in getting across. If thought-disordered people think a great deal without drawing any firm conclusions, depressed people tend to draw conclusions to the exclusion of being able to think very much. They interpret whatever is happening in terms of the same group of ideas: good/bad, strong/weak, lovable/unlovable, and – above all – innocent/guilty, the emphasis always being on the negative of each pair. The conclusions they draw are always the same – that they themselves are responsible for what has happened to them, that they deserved it, and that they can do nothing at all about it. Having reached their own conclusions, they neither want nor need to hear your opinion on the matter. Indeed, in a very real sense they *can't* hear it; the conclusion is so powerful that every other idea or suggestion, however hopeful or positive, is transformed into its opposite by the sheer force of negative conviction.

Writing about depression, Dorothy Rowe says:

This way of seeing the world and oneself does not come into being overnight. It begins with young children having these experiences which teach them to construe themselves as bad. Sometimes children learn this through other people's definitions: 'What a bad boy you really are,' 'You really are an evil little girl.' More often the child decides to see himself or herself as bad rather than endure the greater peril of knowing that the people on whom his safety depends cannot be trusted. 'My good mother punishes me because I am bad.'†

As with schizophrenia, the effort of trying to be the person required by others when the circumstances are particularly difficult results in the distortion of personal communication, and consequently, personality. In schizophrenic thought disorder the world is made meaningless in order to correspond to a person's own experience of failure to make sense of it. In depression, the person distorts his or her image of self in order to keep it congruous with an image of another person which is so precious that it must at all costs be preserved intact. Depressed people appear to be unaffected by all efforts at reassurance as to their personal worth. It's quite hopeless trying to cheer them up. Telling them to 'pull themselves together' is likely to make them feel even worse, even if you do it with the intention of turning their anger outwards, away from themselves and on to you!

At the same time, I have found that many depressed people appreciate your presence, even if they don't seem to do. When you see them again they thank you for having been before, when they weren't feeling well (which they apologize about, of course). Like thought-disordered people, they need to be accepted as people. We may sometimes feel that they are exaggerating their distress, making it more dramatic than it really is in order to gain attention ('She's only acting – don't go wasting your time on her.') Nevertheless, this kind of desperate presentation of despair is part of depression, characteristic of a condition in which you both desperately need and cannot possibly accept reassurance and relief. How can you accept such things if you are engaged in punishing yourself? The suspicion that you're putting on a show makes you feel guiltier than ever ... You are grateful that people care enough

† D. Rowe 'Depression is a Prison' in F. Epting & A. W. Landfeld, *Anticipating Personal Construct Psychology*, University of Nebraska 1985, p. 151.

to sit with you, even though they don't deserve it. Clergy in particular are welcome; if they keep coming even when you ignore them, it shows you can't be *that* bad after all!

The situation is quite different when depressed people begin to get better. When the darkness is starting to lift, clergy can be a great help and comfort as the message of deliverance will be associated with powerful feelings of thankfulness for the lifting of the depression. The Christian conclusions to be drawn from this release from bondage hardly need pointing out. On these occasions, sufferer and minister simply rejoice together.

When somebody who has been well-loved dies, the process of grieving is likely to be both painful and drawn out. In situations where the emotional disturbance is extreme and there seems to be no sign of its reaching an emotional climax and subsiding, bereaved people are frequently referred to psychiatrists, and subsequently diagnosed as suffering from depression. If he or she is willing to spend some time with this kind of patient, who is suffering from unresolved grief rather than any actual psychiatric illness, a minister may find that patience is well-rewarded.

Freda Carter was a fairly active septuagenarian who had continued to take a pride in her appearance and was extremely mentally alert. She had been referred to me by a psychiatrist who, along with her GP, considered that she had developed some symptoms of mental illness as a result of the trauma involved in her husband's death, which had happened twelve years before. I visited Freda each week for a period of several months. During my second visit I began to suspect that her grief for her husband had been reactivated by the loss of her only surviving son, who had recently left home in order to get married. She had managed to cope quite well up to this point, and still appeared to be very much in control of herself. She did feel painfully vulnerable, however: 'As if the whole world's trying to get at me, somehow.' She said that she had 'been all right until Derek (her son) left'. She and Derek had shared the same home, living together and looking after each other. Freda resented her new daughter-in-law fiercely but wouldn't say so until quite late on in the course of interviews. She was new to living alone, although other members of the family gave her a good deal of support. I noticed that the house was in spick-and-span order, just like Freda. She told me that she was used to having to look after things, as her husband had been disabled for many years when he died, and she liked to feel that 'everything was just how it should be – how he wanted it to be'. I asked her about how things had been when her husband was at home. She told me that, because of his disability, her husband had been in charge of their home life, providing the emotional centre to the family – 'If he'd been here, he would have stuck up for me.' Having got this far, Freda managed to say a bit more about her husband each week that I visited her. During the next six months I encouraged her to express a good deal of grief for Donald and also anger over Derek's 'betrayal' on leaving her for another woman. The necessity for preserving an appearance of strength and reliability – being the woman her husband had been so proud of – had prevented her from admitting the presence of such unruly feelings. Despite the inadmissible emotions I encouraged her to express, Freda seemed to value my visits very much. She admitted that most of the time she was unbearably lonely without Donald: 'He was always around, you see.' The depression observed by the doctor expressed itself in extreme protectiveness towards Derek and anger and resentment towards his bride. Feelings like this were completely unacceptable to somebody like her and could only be expressed symbolically, in the form of an extreme defensiveness which originated in a sense of persecuted righteousness. She could not bear to accept her own complicity in the disasters that had overcome her. I tried to give her the personal support and encouragement she needed in order to accept feelings of anger and jealousy which prevented her coming to terms with the mistakes she felt herself to have actually made. By the time I

finally stopped visiting her Freda had made real progress both
in forgiving and being forgiven.

The purpose of these two rather lengthy excursions into
describing actual mental illnesses is to underline an essential
point about Christian ministry to the mentally disturbed
which is this: *the ministry is about listening*. This is really
very important indeed. If you want to be a healer you have
to learn how to listen. If this doesn't come easily – and in fact
it doesn't to a great many people – it is a good idea to take it
seriously enough to be systematic about it: Michael Jacobs
has written several books, and they are mentioned in the
bibliography. People with either schizophrenia or depression
are helped by the regard another person shows them by really
listening to them, and so are patients with other kinds of
psychiatric problem. Those suffering from mania, for
example, who tend to want you to do all sorts of things for
them, and to rush off and do them *now*; or anxious people
needing calmness and reassurance. There are some situations
in which listening is the only constructive thing you can do.
The intense central phase of depression is one of these.
Another is obsessionality, the total domination of a person's
mind by a particular idea which rules all their behaviour. The
difficulty here is to avoid the temptation to try and convince
the deluded person that they are wrong, that they cannot be
right. This is an impossible job, at least under the circumstances of *ordinary conversation*, as it invariably dis-
tresses them and gets you nowhere at all. They look at you as
if the problem were yours, not theirs. In a sense they are right;
why are you working so hard to convince another person that
he or she is not experiencing what they can actually feel
themselves going through? By listening, however, you can
help someone to look at themselves 'in the round' so that they
may eventually feel secure enough, with your respect and
approval, to pay more regard to the unpersecuted parts of
themselves, helping them to grow gradually strong enough to

master the obsession from inside. Psychiatrists find obsession-ality very hard to treat. It doesn't respond at all well to tablets, and there isn't really time for lengthy conversions. People suffering from this awful burden often seek out a minister and, so long as he resists the urge to argue, value the opportunity to talk to him.

A similar situation exists with regard to the reality-disturbing effects of schizophrenia. Normal psychiatric procedure requires that delusions, whether they be 'voices in the head' or visual hallucinations, should never be taken as a part of objective reality, either by the people suffering from them or those trying to help them. It is acceptable and proper to explain to the sufferer that you understand that the delusion is real, that he or she is *really* hearing, seeing, smelling, feeling these things. What you should not do is allow yourself to be drawn into his or her private scenario and pretend that you hear, see, smell, feel these things too. Strangely enough it is quite easy to do this; the patient's experience is so vivid and your own urge to 'get alongside' and really share whatever it may be that she or he is going through combine to get the better of your judgment, and you find yourself in that hazardous territory in which emotional support may easily become confused with intellectual assent. A particular kind of listening is called for in such cases, one which makes as clear as possible the precise nature of the support you are offering. You have to get across the fact that you aren't questioning the presence of the delusion, nor the misery it causes, only its independent existence. Whatever it is is part of them. Your concern is for the whole person, voices and all.

Listed below are some notes on recognizing the symptoms and signs of mental illness.

A. *Psychosis* (Behaviour that is qualitatively abnormal)

It is very important to understand that these are evidence of acute or active forms of illness. If anyone in the congregation is unfortunate enough to show any of these signs or describe any of the symptoms their GP or Community Psychiatric Nurse should be consulted. It is at least likely that they haven't been keeping up with their medication.

Hallucinations Things experienced when they are not there. (People may hear voices discussing them etc. The hallucinations of people suffering from dementia or delirium typically consist of noises of banging.)

Delusions False beliefs, held to despite the evidence. (e.g. 'Cancer is contagious'; 'I am being controlled from outer space.'); obsessional ideas.

Disordered thinking Ideas loosely associated with parts of the argument omitted to the detriment of the sense; rapid thinking without ideas being 'properly finished'.

Inappropriate mood The content of what is said is at odds with the manner of delivery.

All these signs and symptoms are usually associated with *schizophrenia*, but they are also found in acute *depressive states*, such as those signified by

Withdrawal from social contact Reduced productivity, neglect of personal appearance.

Physical and mental slowing Loss of appetite, hypochondriacal ideas, constipation, insomnia.

Delusional ideas Deriving from normal fears. (In its depressed form this may lead to the idea that one's body may actually be decaying etc.)

Elated mood Physical over-activity, rapid but unclear thinking. Associated with the manic phase of *manic depressive illness* in which mania and depression alternate.

B. *Neurosis* (Behaviour that is quantitatively abnormal)

Psychiatric conditions that hide behind physical states are less straightforward – i.e. harder to identify.

Hysteria and *Anxiety* are examples of defensive neuroses. Hysteria is associated with the attempt to escape from intolerable ideas or memories by locating their discomfort else-where, i.e. in actual physical pains or disabilities. Symptoms of hysteria may include blindness, deafness, anaesthesia, pain etc. Sometimes GPs dismiss these conditions after having performed the obvious physical tests.

Obsessional neurosis is rare but frightening – an idea or feeling that takes on a compulsive force and shows itself in phobias and private rituals.

Anxiety disorders can be generalized, phobic or panic. Gen-eralized anxiety is expressed in feelings of fear and dread which are global and all-pervasive; phobic anxiety is an irrational fear provoked by particular objects or situations; panic attacks are separate episodes of fear. They are all associ-ated with the normal flight/fight response; somehow or other this has become too easily triggered off. Generally speaking, people suffering from these things want to hide them, believ-ing that they ought to be able to cope with what they know 'is silly'. They, too, need professional help; or help guided by a professional. The GP will refer them to a clinical psychologist who will help them to unlearn these ways of reacting by teaching them alternative ways of dealing with aversive situ-ations. The symptoms associated with schizophrenia, however, need a different approach. Very probably the person concerned will be unable to recognize that they need help. In these situations the CPN may be consulted directly, without waiting to consult the GP. Every family practice has one or more Community Psychiatric Nurse attached to it, and the system is organized to deliver help as quickly and efficiently as possible.

This account is necessarily a brief one; you would have to read a lot more if you wanted to be sure that you could always tell whether or not an individual was actually suffering from mental illness. Behaviour has to be extremely well-developed before it is safe to attempt to base a psychiatric diagnosis on it. Certainly, the purpose of talking about these things is to provide some help for those who come into contact with people who are or have been psychiatrically ill. At the most primitive level they need to know when to consult the doctor. What I have written may be of some use; perhaps it will encourage people to go further into the subject and read one of the many text books that are available.

What is more important, however, is that men and women who have been, or still are, psychiatric patients should be allowed to get better. That they should not be considered ill simply because they are themselves – because they come from 'that place'. If they don't behave in any of these ways they are unlikely to be ill. Not being ill, they don't need special treatment and won't thank you for giving it them. They want to be allowed to be themselves. Some of them certainly are keen to put being a patient behind them and should be allowed to do so. If things start to get hard again they will almost certainly be relieved that you have some idea about the kind of thing that can go wrong and that you know what to do about it.

Can mentally ill people respond to language about God? Certainly, mental handicap does not mean inability to believe in God. Many mentally handicapped people I have known have had a good deal of faith. In fact they have provided me with very real support in my ministry. Belief in God seems to be what the psychologists call an 'independent variable'. You do not need to be clever to have it, nor does being clever prevent you from having it. With some people who are suffering from mental illness, it can lead to very strange conclusions; but these represent the effect of disorder of thought upon a basic underlying faith, they distort it but do not invalidate it. Other mentally ill people will tell you that they once believed, but because of their present condition, do so no longer. God, they say, has punished them by taking the gift of faith away. This is very dramatic and, at the time, tragic, because it is so firmly believed. I have often had reason to thank God that this state of mind – or of heart – is often not permanent and that faith returns; but while it exists it is completely intransigent, however much you reassure and exhort. Urging somebody to feel something which they once felt but feel no longer only makes them feel more guilty, more rejected than ever. You simply become part of that self that rejects itself, contributing to the depression you strive to relieve. Better to pray silently, hold a hand (if this is permissible), and wait. Try to sit next to someone rather than opposite them so that you are alongside rather than in any position they can construe as challenging.

Conversely, when trying to come to grips with the convoluted religious ideas of people diagnosed as having schizophrenia, it is important to sit opposite them and to concentrate hard on what they are saying, however difficult it may be, so that you may bestow some kind of interpersonal reality on their ideas by simply trying to understand them. Because it is so hard to get on the right wavelength with people who think and talk like this – who often seem to be thinking and talking in order *not* to be understood, as a kind of defence against contact with the person listening – there is a temptation simply to give up and move away. I have found, however, that when I really try to discover the main point that is being made underneath the smokescreen of examples and irrelevancies, my efforts are often rewarded, to our mutual delight. This way of talking can become habitual, so that when the person really wants to communicate he or she finds they can't. They are unable to say anything 'straight' any more. Try to have time to help. Listen to what the person wants to say rather than simply taking note of the 'mad' way it is being said.

You don't have to speak to mentally ill people in a special way. They understand what you mean if you talk the way you normally do. Nobody likes to be talked down to, so try not to do this. There is a subtle difference between choosing your words carefully in order to be understood by people with a limited linguistic code, which applies to many if not all mentally handicapped people, and presenting what you have to say in a condescending way as if you were talking to people you consider stupid. You are in the business of communication, and it is up to you to find ways of doing this efficiently, which means without unsettling people more than you can help.

Probably the most important thing about recognizing psychiatric illness is knowing the difference between psychosis and neurosis. This centres round what psychiatrists call insight. Most people use this word to mean 'the ability to understand others'; here it means knowing that one is thinking or feeling abnormally oneself, and need help. The main symptom of psychosis is usually considered to be lack of ability to see oneself as ill. Neurotic people, however, are quite sure there is something the matter. The symptoms of psychosis tend to be more dramatic – hearing voices in the head, attempting suicide, violent changes of mood etc. – whereas neurosis usually expresses itself in ways that seem to other people to be simply exaggerations of normal behaviour, as in extreme anxiety, obsessional states, various ways of over-reacting to the stresses and strains of life.

Both groups of people need assistance. Strangely enough, neurotic people are in some ways harder to help than psychotic ones, even though they appear to be – and almost certainly are – less 'ill'. The differences lie in the length and intensity of disturbance. Psychosis tends to occur in well-defined episodes. It occurs suddenly and then suddenly departs. In between, however, it certainly makes its presence felt, and it needs specialist treatment. Because of the patient's lack of insight about his or her condition the treatment aims at re-establishing some kind of chemical balance within the brain. Psychiatrists find it very hard, or even impossible, to sustain the kind of therapeutic exchange of ideas and feelings on which psychotherapy depends.

Psychotherapy uses relationship in order to restore someone's ability to relate. Because this ability goes back a lifetime and its roots are in early childhood, the process of rebuilding may take a long time. This is why I said that neurosis was often more difficult to 'cure' than psychosis. Phobic conditions, which are usually classified as neurotic, are often effectively removed by techniques of desensitization, according to which the sufferer is gradually, by very small increments, brought into contact with whatever it is that they find terrifying until they are able to deal with it without panicking. This is a process that takes weeks, rather than years. Most neurotic complaints take longer.

Generally speaking psychotherapy is reserved for neurotic people (if they are lucky enough to be able to afford it – very little is available from the Health Service), because they are considered to be able to benefit from discovering the unconscious reasons for their behaviour. On the other hand, psychotherapists give examples of people suffering from psychosis who have gained insight as a result of psychotherapy, and learned to come to terms with their symptoms as a stage in conquering them.

It is worth remembering that behaviour which seems odd to us may not appear so to them. Indeed, there may not seem to be anything wrong! So long as other people are not distressed by their symptoms, they can be left alone. There may, of course, come a time when some kind of intervention is necessary, for their sake as well as other people's. Perhaps they see themselves as innocent victims of a plot, devised upon another planet but infiltrating the congregation with devastating effect ... Obviously it is difficult to get someone who believes this to seek help.

Modern psychiatric medication is very effective in dealing with this kind of thing, although a certain amount of manoeuvring has to take place in order to persuade the person involved to accept it. If you're not very careful you find yourself cast as part of the conspiracy. It is a situation that Community Psychiatric Nurses are familiar with, however.

People suffering from paranoia, a kind of schizophrenia characterized by ideas that they are the victim of some kind of personal plot, tend to find some things about religion particularly fascinating and also very frightening. Ideas like heaven and hell, alternative realities having an effect on human life, different 'spheres of being' influencing this world are rapidly translated by paranoid people into terms of an inescapable destiny, the work of an avenging God who is everywhere and in charge of everything, and who chooses individuals in order to damn them. If you tend to think in terms of life being 'out to get you' then you are probably open to this kind of religious idea. Pastors, and Christians in general, need to remember that even the very best, most hopeful message can be misinterpreted by someone who is only able to construe things in one way. You don't need to use theological arguments to minister God's love.

The same kind of process of translation happens when we talk to depressed people about forgiveness. The message we set out to deliver isn't the one they receive. It's as if they *can't* receive it. It may be true, they say, in fact I'm sure it's true, but it isn't true *about me*. They weep and you feel you have made them feel worse. Once 'out of the valley' they remember how kind you were, and even sometimes what you said. At the time it seemed useless, a 'waste of effort', but in fact it wasn't. I am convinced that, with regard to depression, at some level or other, the message gets through, though not at the time. Perhaps it's also true of paranoia. But the main message is simply, be there.

6

Listening

There are two main categories of ex-patient; those who are still receiving active psychiatric treatment and attend a psychiatric clinic or are visited at home by a Community Psychiatric Nurse, and those who are leading normal lives independent of psychiatric supervision (although they may well be taking drugs of one kind or another). Both groups are likely to be lonely and disorientated, at least during their first months. The idea of life within the community may be attractive if you have spent a long time yearning to get out of hospital but, once out, the community can be a pretty draughty place. If you have been part of a supportive group of friends within the hospital then you will find it even draughtier. If years of playing the system have rendered you ward-wise, a prominent and influential figure in patient society, the sheer powerlessness of your present position is likely to prove intolerable – like being a Company Sergeant Major one minute and a Night Security Guard the next. This kind of reversal happens to most people at some time or another, usually when they leave school or when they retire. In the case of an ex-patient, however, it is greatly exaggerated. Some of the men and women have spent forty or fifty years in the same job.

Both groups need advice and help, although the second need it much more than the first as they no longer receive regular psychiatric support (except of a chemical kind). In fact, this may not turn out to be such a drawback. Clergy are often nervous about interfering in the treatment of people who are still 'seeing the psychiatrist'. If they consult the psychiatrist themselves, he or she is very likely to say that the kind of support they are able to give is precisely the kind that the person needs. Psychiatrically vulnerable people need social support of a non-compulsory kind. In addition, they need an opportunity to talk over their problems with someone who will take them seriously. Because their problems tend to concern the experience of being human, they are looking for someone to talk to who is willing to discuss the meaning of life. This is something that most psychiatrists hold to be outside their remit. They have neither the skill nor the time.

It is not, however, outside ours. It is precisely our job. The message about life's meaning that we bear is precisely the message they need to hear. Everywhere and always our job is to communicate the love of God. This is our healing skill. In fact, of course, the skill belongs to God, and we only draw attention to it, and by so doing make people more aware of its presence and activity amongst us. In other words, we 'minister' the love of God. We may do this through strength as the Father, or weakness as the Son, or in the impossible way followed by the Holy Spirit. Our task is to find the way that is appropriate for reaching the tortured person that has come to us for help and to let the light of Christ through. This light may suffuse the world, set the heavens on fire, or shine like a tiny candle in the corner of an immense hall. The principle is the same: the right light for the right person at the right time.

If you want to help the mentally ill your prayer will always be for understanding and insight so that you might hit on the particular approach for the particular patient. Everybody is different, and it is precisely within the areas of their difference that their disturbance is located. At the same time there are some general principles. The only way you will communicate with someone who is deeply depressed is wordlessly, by holding hands if they will let you. Schizophrenic people will tend to want to talk at great length, and not always intelligibly, but you must make your point about God's total love simply and definitely, and with the utmost conviction: 'Come to me all you who labour and are overburdened, and I will give you rest.' Keep saying it until you are sure the message has really sunk in. Anxious people, who would like so much to fit in with what you suggest but are so preoccupied that you feel they are never really listening, need the assurance of Christ's presence as something infinitely more important than anything else in the world: 'and know that I am always with you: yes, to the end of time.' If you can't get the words across, think in terms of finding a way of transmitting the same message obliquely, using stories, plays or pictures. I have heard of some congregations using dolls or puppets to embody the vital messages of acceptance.

Most important of all, however, is for *you* to listen to *them*. When we consider the ministry of listening in its psychiatric version we come very near the role of the minister as healer. First of all, however, we must look at the importance of the pastoral counsellor. Clergy are invariably expected to be counsellors as well as spiritual guides; in other words, they are not only expected to listen to people with religious difficulties and give them appropriate encouragement and advice, but to be able and willing to help anybody with any kind of non-medical problem, whether or not they lay claim to any religious belief. There is nothing particularly strange in this, of course. Most clergy are used to being as helpful and supportive as they can be, in whatever situation they find themselves. Actually, the kind of listening I have been describing is very like the counselling I found myself teaching nurses when I worked as a chaplain in a large psychiatric hospital. This was one of those commissions that chaplains are likely to attract wherever they happen to be working. It could have been 'The Care of the Dying' or 'Helping the Bereaved' – indeed, it frequently was – but it was considered equally appropriate for the chaplain's help to be sought with regard to counselling, because clergy are commonly thought of as people who know how to give verbal help to those in trouble. On one of my visits to the nursing school I had dropped a few hints to the effect that I might have something to offer in this connection, and very soon afterwards I received a letter from the head of the school asking me if I would consider talking to nursing students – 'An Introduction to Counselling' or any other title I might prefer. I said I would be happy to do so, and so began an association with the nursing school that lasted many years.

I expected to be talking to a few groups of students at a time. I can remember vividly how nervous I felt when I found myself confronted with a large lecture theatre full of students. What I actually said on that occasion I can't remember, but I know it was based on the seven 'Principles of Counselling' outlined by Felix Biestek, a priest/pastoral counsellor, whose approach seems to be to be ideally suited to the kind of counselling which can be undertaken by people who have received little or no formal training but are often called upon to give comfort and support to others. Biestek's principles, however, function at all levels of professional expertise, being laws rather than techniques: it is up to the individual to find his or her own ways of putting them into practice. Like all laws, however, it is better to observe them inexpertly rather than ignore them completely. I find them helpful in my own practice and pass them on to those who have not yet come into contact with them. (The principles are Biestek's, the comments my own:)

1. *Individuation*   This is not used here as the name of a subtle and pervasive process of psychic development, although the state of mind required by the principle will certainly help you become more yourself! Individuation here means treating the other person in ways that show you regard them as unique individuals. In practical terms, counsellors should not say things like 'You students are all the same', or 'patients are always coming here and saying what you said,' or even 'I

know all about doctors!' This is a very practical rule; no one is going to confide in you if they get the impression that you regard them as a 'typical case' of whatever it may be. As a corollary, personal autobiography is to be very carefully handled. It doesn't really help the unique person sitting opposite to know that you were 'just the same at your age'. By all means draw on your own experience, but be careful not to use it to blot out your client's.

2. *Purposeful expression of feeling* This refers to the client and means exactly what it says. The expression of feeling leads to the clarification of ideas and intentions to the extent that the avoidance of feeling has involved the avoidance of the thoughts that accompany it. Most, if not all, psychopathologies – ways of explaining emotional problems – take account of our human ability to ignore the pressure of thoughts and feelings that cause us discomfort. If a client is visibly moved this is usually a sign that he or she is becoming aware of something she or he would rather not remember. If the things which provide the key to the present problem lie in this painful area, the process of uncovering them is bound to hurt. Nevertheless, the feelings have a purpose: we avoid the urge to look away and say 'Come, come, don't cry.' By crying, our client may come to see what he or she had carefully avoided seeing, but what they need to see in order to understand the present problem. Some people cry very easily, and use their tears as a way of avoiding having to confront the real issue which faces them. These easily produced tears may be intended to dissuade the counsellor from pursuing the path he or she has entered upon – they are a sign that something at a rather deeper level needs to be looked at. The real tears, the ones that come unbidden, show that important disclosures may be at hand.

3. *Limited self-involvement* The suggestion here is that you cannot possibly help anybody who has any kind of emotional problem unless you are willing to involve yourself in their experience to the extent of using your imagination in

order to 'see things with their eyes'. The word that comes to mind here is empathy. Empathy has been called 'understanding with the heart'. This seems to me to be a very good definition. The practical thing about empathy is that you cannot understand the reason for anybody's behaviour unless you have some idea of the *quality* of their experience; you cannot convince them of your goodwill without providing evidence that you understand them, and this evidence can only be obtained from the inside, via imagination working upon common humanity. The impractical thing about it is that it is possible for sensitive people to become *too* involved, to be taken over by another's distress to such an extent that they can see the situation through their eyes only – in which case they are not going to be very good at helping them find a solution to the problem confronting them.

4. *Acceptance*   This, too, means what it says. It appears to be the easiest and most obvious of the seven principles until you realize that it isn't only people but ideas and attitudes you are being asked to make room for. In a very real sense, people's opinions are *part* of them – from your point of view, a very important part, because they represent the way in which they organize the world they live in. Wherever I go, whether I am at home, at work, or enjoying time off with my friends, I take my opinions and attitudes with me in order to interpret the meaning, gauge the significance, of everything that happens to me. It follows from this that my problems and difficulties very much colour my attitudes to events; and everybody who professes concern for me must pay due regard to the value those attitudes have for me. Attitudes which are personally limiting or anti-social can be changed, of course, and this is certainly the object of some kinds of counselling. The principle of acceptance, however, directs us towards a willingness to allow people to retain ideas, attitudes and prejudices which we ourselves do not share and which may even sometimes horrify and appal us, and, while not taking the same view of them, to accept the fact that they are very

important to the person concerned. Obviously this is a very
hard thing to do, particularly if you are a clergyman; and this
is one of the points at which counselling – which really means
not counselling – parts company with spiritual direction.
Since, however, you have to accept something as real before
you can possibly hope to change it, the difference may not be
so great after all.

5. *Non-judgmental attitude*   A hard one for people with
firm views about the rightness or wrongness of things. I think
it was St Augustine who said that 'To know all is to forgive
all.' It was certainly Jesus who said 'Judge not, that ye be not
judged.' One of the purposes of counselling technique is to
find out what is going on for the person you are counselling.
There may be a lot you can find out by observation of body
language or by interpreting things that your client says on
other, more general matters; but your main source of information will always be the things she or he says about *her or
himself* – the material the client or patient presents to you in
order that you may know what kind of people they are. Their
purpose in talking about themselves is not only to put you in
the picture with regard to their personal circumstances, but
to enlist your goodwill and make sure you will be 'on their
side' in whatever situation it may be that confronts them. In
other words, they wish to *commend* themselves. If they don't
manage to do this, they will go somewhere else and you will
have lost the chance of helping them.

A good deal of effort must be spent, therefore, in resisting
the impulse to argue about things on which you yourself
hold strong views. If you think somebody is wrong about
something, make sure that they regard you as a friendly,
concerned human being before you reveal the fact to them.
On no account be in a hurry to let them know how you feel.
If you wait, you may give yourself time to get to understand
factors of temperament, background and personal history
that have contributed to his or her looking at life the way
they do, and you will also be prevented from pre-empting the

outcome of the interview by indulging your own need to 'sort people out'. No one is going to ask your help if they suspect you of having condemned them in advance. If there are things you feel you must say, as a Christian counsellor, then you must be patient, and wait until it is possible to 'speak the truth in love' and be heard in the mutuality of acceptance.

6. *Client self-determination* You are not there to tell people what to do, or to make them feel guilty for not doing it. This is the foundation stone of counselling. Counselling is about freedom. Its rise to prominence during the last fifty years coincides with a growing awareness of the part played by personal autonomy within the achievement of human maturity. The relationship between counsellor and counselled must be, to use the categories of Transactional Analysis, an 'adult' ↔ 'adult' interaction. The counsellor is no longer a 'parent' nor the client a 'child'; this particular conformation is to be avoided if at all possible.

This is the second principal difference between counselling and spiritual direction. In its traditional form spiritual direction depends entirely upon the manipulation of parent/child roles. As in Freudian psychotherapy memories of childhood dependence, when guilt, anger and shame played so powerful a part of our awareness, are revived in terms of present experience and transformed by becoming part of a renewed experience of relationship with a father or mother. This is certainly part of a minister's role in his or her specifically religious identity and function. In my opinion, however, it is not a counselling role. I agree with Biestek that pastoral counselling depends on the assertion of a client's freedom to make choices that are, as far as possible, uninfluenced by the need to please father figures of any kind, secular or religious.

7. *Confidentiality* It hardly needs pointing out that a chaplain has a clear-cut duty of confidentiality. Pastoral counselling and spiritual direction coincide here. People expect to have their confidences respected: both doctors and ministers adhere to a rule of confidentiality. At the same time the growth of

interdisciplinary teamwork is threatening to some of those to whom we offer our services, who suspect that in order to work efficiently in such circumstances a good deal of information must be handed round a large number of people. Some counsellors in some settings – nurses, teachers and social workers in particular – have to tell their clients that there may be some things that they will have to tell their own superiors. They must tell them this beforehand, of course, if they hope to retain the trust of those clients; once something has been disclosed it is open to the counsellor's assessment as to whether or not it must go 'further up the line'. This was a matter that attracted a good deal of discussion among the nurses at my lectures and workshops. A ward sister who, while counselling a student nurse, learnt an item of information which affected the safety of patients in the hospital, would be bound to report it. This being so, what was the point of the confidentiality rule? We decided that, since counselling was not the confessional, there was no need to disclose everything to the counsellor. A certain amount of circumstantial vagueness was acceptable so long as the emotional truth was preserved.

In short, then, Biestek's principles bring home a very important fact about our role as pastoral counsellors. We are not there to answer questions in the sense of giving guidance, but to encourage people to ask and answer their own questions. A counsellor acts very like a mirror, reflecting a positive image of the patient or client, reinforcing her or his sense of being a person, adding to it a spiritual awareness, supplied by the counsellor, of being a worthwhile person. As we saw, this sense of worth does not come from what the counsellor says but from the way he or she accepts not simply what the other says, but what he or she is.

This is very important indeed. Two writers among very many have developed this notion of acceptance and encouragement. The first is Carl Rogers, the inventor of 'client-centred therapy'. This is a psychotherapeutic approach which tries to help people regain their lost emotional balance by accepting those aspects of themselves that are frightened, angry, ashamed and generally cause pain to the self and reincorporating them within their conscious personality. This is more or less the aim of all psychotherapy, of course. The main difference is that Rogerian counsellors aim to encourage their clients by convincing them of their real worth as people so that they can themselves develop the 'positive self-regard' which can reincorporate those areas of self that have been disavowed and denied. To this end Carl Rogers worked towards developing 'a therapeutic orientation which relies primarily upon the capacity of the client'.

One aspect of the client's capacity is the innate tendency to search for meaning in life, what Viktor Frankl identifies as the religious tendency characteristic of the entire human species. The therapist recognizes the need to ask questions as well as try to answer them: 'patients ask "what's the purpose?", "what's it worth?"'. This questioning starts at the very beginning of therapy as patients wonder why, unhappy and disillusioned as they are, they should bother attending to the therapist. More to the point, why should he or she bother with them? This basic kind of interest in getting better is evidence of an intrinsic reaching out for personal help in making sense of life, because the urge to meaning is the basis of psychological wholeness. The urge towards, not the possession of: how else could Frankl and his fellow prisoners have survived the death camps in Nazi Germany?

Rogers and Frankl, though differing in other ways, provide evidence of the need for acceptance and encouragement which is our main justification in the sphere of pastoral counselling. The symbolic importance of the minister or priest epitomizes Frankl's purpose because it embodies the search for meaning and so is healing in itself: Rogers, on the other hand, shows how we may curb the desire to direct and dominate and, by reflecting others upon themselves, heal by reinforcement of the self. With Biestek, these constitute three ways of approaching pastoral counselling, chosen because they are particularly appropriate for psychiatric work. The counselling approach may be developed as far as you wish, in as many directions as you find helpful – please don't let me limit you. You may wish to follow an entirely different model of counselling. I have described Biestek's because it is the one I use, and because it has particular relevance for some aspects of the minister's role within the healing team. It is just structured enough: more direction and the counsellor runs the risk of increasing his or her client's pathology by making them more anxious, guilt-ridden or paranoid; less structure and she or he may appear to be providing no more than friendship and spiritual support.

Rogers and Frankl bring us into the area of actual psycho-therapy in which the priest or minister is seen as an actual healer, one who uses special religious gifts and skills for therapeutic purposes. It is vitally important that you should be clearly seen to be a Christian priest or minister. By this I mean that your specific role within the healing team is that of a Christian healer. The psychological understanding that you possess will be used by you as a means for Christian healing. As a Christian minister or priest you will need to find a way of approaching sick people which does not get in the way of the healing effect of your message – which actually increases the message's clarity and impact by helping people to hear it and be affected by it. The message is to be delivered clearly, as itself, not in any disguised psychological form.

Having said that, you will find that some background psychological and psychiatric understanding will enable you to avoid erecting barriers when your aim is to clear pathways. People suffering from psychiatric illness are not easy to communicate with in ordinary conversation. The ways in which they defend themselves from emotional pain distort the message they want to convey; and yet those distortions are clung on to because the pain involved somehow atones for the pain avoided. Priests and ministers, above all, wish to deliver their message of God's forgiveness and their own friendship and desire to understand. I have always found, however, that a head-on approach has an alienating effect on the patient, who is firmly entrenched in his or her own way of interpreting everything that happens. It is quite possible, in this private world, for love to be a code word for hate, or even to refer to someone else altogether. 'Poor chaplain, she doesn't know what she's talking about!' 'He's a good man, he has no idea that Satan is talking through him . . . '

Whatever may be said about their causes, these ideas are deeply entrenched. Guided by George Kelly's 'personal construct psychology' I have learned another approach to the attempt to make contact.

The personal construct approach regards behaviour which is strange and abnormal as a way of making sense of the world that no longer works properly. Human behaviour, both thinking and feeling, is only practical, only really 'works', when it is in a process of change; and it can only change when the person concerned is able to reinterpret the situation confronting and surrounding her. Kelly said that people are their own scientists, perpetually experimenting with possible ways of anticipating the future in the light of the past. What is equally important is that the therapist, too, is a scientist, following up each hypothesis suggested by the patient, changing his overall view of the client whenever he receives new information. Because everything we know is connected, when one part changes the whole web is affected. This is our personal construct 'system'. Its aim is to relate new information to what we are already using in order to anticipate events correctly. We need to be able to do this in a workmanlike fashion in order to cope with whatever it may be that will happen next; in other words, in order to keep on changing while remaining ourselves.

The therapist's aim is the same as that of his fellow scientist, the patient – that of achieving significant changes, changes that have real effects – in systems that resist change. To put this another way, we might use the more familiar language of personal relationship. In order to 'have a relationship' with somebody else we must be able to imagine what it must be like to be in their situation; what it would be like, in fact, to *be* them. We have to construe their personal world by taking it into our own. Drama is the best example of the use of 'as if' to promote human relationship, but in fact everybody does it all the time. When we perform this act of personal acceptance, acceptance of somebody else's world *as they see it themselves*, our own world changes. This does not mean that we are completely converted to their way of seeing, nor they to ours, but that a degree of sharing is achieved. To a greater or lesser degree, our worlds are changed.

The actual information contained in the messages exchanged in this way may be confusing to both sides. So far as mental illness is concerned, both therapists and patient will have difficulty in achieving the 'as if' state which permits the sharing of worlds. Two sources of difficulty immediately come to mind. If my personal construct system is rigorously organized and consequently resistant to change, I will have difficulty in adapting to anybody else's point of view, even within the brackets provided by 'as if'. On the other hand, if my system is very loosely organized, new ideas and viewpoints may have difficulty in finding a firm foothold in the shifting sand of my vague interpretation of the world. These are extreme ways of construing which personal construct psychology associates with people diagnosed as obsessional, depressed or paranoid on the one hand, or suffering from schizophrenic thought disorder or various kinds of dementia on the other.

Our ordinary ways of making sense of one another suffer less extreme hang-ups, however. For instance, we become anxious when faced with a situation which is so new that we can't predict the actions of other people and so have no way of telling how we should behave; we fear that our construct system will turn out in the event to be inadequate. If the foundations of our world-view seem to be threatened by a state of affairs which goes against something very basic to a core role, (i.e. to one of the most important ways in which we see ourselves acting in relation to others), we experience a kind of blocking in our ability to relate and consequently, to change. If, on the other hand, we are conscious of having somehow betrayed one (and, by implication, all) of these 'core roles' which guide our life, we feel extreme guilt. This has the effect of making us distrust the value of our entire construct system: if the centre proves untrustworthy, what good will the rest be? To cling on to ways of making sense of life which have been shown to be ineffective or even destructive is an effort to resist personal change which goes against the basis of relationship; there can be no relationship without mutual adaptation and change. This kind of hostile defensiveness leads to the decay of the qualities of understanding and sensitivity which someone possessed before they abandoned the possibility of becoming right by turning their backs on being wrong.

These are all ways in which a way of looking at life designed to allow development at the same time as preserving identity may cease to function in the way it should. The kind of personal change involved here is fundamental to human relationships. Wherever people meet, the situation for each individual person always changes; without change of any kind, there is no real personal encounter, for we always, in one way or another, affect one another. Mental illnesses are an obvious barrier to this kind of encounter; for either in their cause or their effect they represent a breakdown of the ability to communicate and so to change the situation. In every therapeutic relationship there are at least two people. If the one designated as patient finds difficulty in communicating, a good deal of the responsibility for getting through falls on the other people involved.

One way of doing this is by breaking down some of the barriers to communication by approaching the problem from quite a different angle, one which is not so concerned to understand directly, but allows sense to emerge from nonsense in the way that reality emerges from a game. Kelly suggests ways in which this may be attempted, based upon one central change-inducing approach. Kelly described a 'creative cycle' which characterizes our experience of change. This is a transition from 'loosened construing' – when things don't make much sense to us, and we have abandoned our ability to make precise predictions about the future – to 'tightened construing', when things have fallen into place and we can make plans to deal with whatever is likely to happen next. The transition itself is always the crucial part of the process because it has neither looseness nor tightness, relaxation nor concentration, but a chaotic mixture of both ... This is the mixture from which understanding emerges and in which relationships are born.

My years as a psychiatric chaplain made me extremely interested in the essential 'area between', when the past is over and the future not yet begun. Time and again I found that my place was in and around chaos, on the edge of things. This is not to say that I set out to create chaos, although it may sometimes have seemed like that. On the contrary, my role was to control chaos by expressing it: I tried to give official recognition to the presence of kinds of human truthfulness that were explicitly denied by the clear statements of attitude and intention made by the institution. It was around the chaplain that the 'on the other hands', the 'more to it than this's', the 'I wouldn't start from here's' gathered. As the representative of truth which declares itself to be divine no pastor can avoid producing chaos in places like those, where truth is strictly defined and meaning clearly stated.

All the same, the chaplain does not actually set out to induce chaos, simply to be himself and do his job. There are cases where real institutional chaos has been created by a chaplain who has identified too closely with one or other professional groupings within the team, thus interfering with the balance that his or her presence is intended to maintain. Mostly, however, the chaplain's presence within the institution proclaims the questionable nature of official truth in an official way. He or she cannot avoid being chaotic. People in the process of undergoing transition may seek the chaplain out as somebody who will tolerate them as they are, containing their shattered unity without denying its personal significance. Real personal change is an expression of human creativity: in his or her relationship with psychiatric patients, a chaplain will encounter instances of the emergence of emotional and intellectual states which are totally different from the ones that preceded them. For new ideas and intentions to emerge the stranglehold exerted by old ones must be loosened. The chaplain's contribution to this creative kind of chaos can, I believe, be crucial.

Andrew had been through several training schemes since leaving school at sixteen. He had a supportive mother and father and one small sister. For several months after leaving school Andrew had 'hung around' with a group of mates, all more or less his own age, and all male. His parents had not approved of his companions, considering them 'rough', a judgment shared by Andrew himself: 'They hadn't a clue.' Perhaps they sensed that this was basically his opinion because he gradually lost touch with them, so that by the time his YTS was over he had no friends at all. I met him when he had just begun to attend a psychiatric clinic after a failed suicide attempt. We struck up a conversation, and I invited him to come and see me if he felt lonely. Andrew thanked me; he did feel lonely, desperately so. That was why he had attempted suicide; perhaps someone would take the initiative and make friends with him. He had a feeling it had been a mistake, however: 'They'll think me a nut now, so no one'll come near me. I mess everything up!'

I saw Andrew on and off for several months, usually at the clinic. I was surprised to find him older than I thought he was – much older than he looked. He was a fine pianist. Indeed, playing the piano was the one great interest in his life. I should have liked to hear him play but the opportunity rarely presented itself. He would have liked to have made a career of his music and practised hard all through his childhood. Unfortunately his parents, although encouraging him to play, refused to see his music as anything but a hobby: 'You have to be good, very good, impossibly good ...' An unlucky fit of nerves during the Advanced Grade of the Associated Board exams put an end to his own ideas of a professional career, to his parents' relief. When I met him he was still 'tinkling around', not doing very much, just keeping his hand in, usually with music that was much too hard for him to play – music which to play properly, you would have to be 'impossibly good'.

Actually, I don't think he played much at all. He certainly liked to talk about it though. When he came to me he would lean back in his chair and grin and talk about Alkan. I am an amateur pianist, and so I knew what he was talking about. If I hadn't he would not have come. He was lucky to have found someone who spoke his language – and spoke it safely.

This certainly got us off to a good start. At the second session I got him to write what Kelly calls a 'self-characterization': 'Andrew is a problem to his parents. He can't stick at anything. He has no abilities and only one talent. People often accuse him of exaggeration; he can do the ordinary things, of course, and got on pretty well at school. He would have gone to university, but there didn't seem to be any point because you need to have some idea of what you want to do with your life afterwards. He used to be good at music and is still very interested in it. Andrew seems to have failed at deciding what sort of person he is, or wants to be. At the moment he has no real friends. He can't seem to get interested in any of the boring things in which they are interested. Perhaps he could if he could only try harder. There is nothing at all he can stick at.'

I pointed out that all this seemed a bit negative. He was certainly very good indeed at being negative. It seemed to be something he could really stick at. Perhaps he ought to give master classes in negativity. I suggested we play a game in which a very depressed Beethoven explained his reasons for not writing music. Andrew was a bit put out by this suggestion but soon saw its potential for hilarity – at one point he strolled over to the piano and began to play part of Opus 103 while pantomiming deep despair. Our sessions together were usually like this, a mixture of hilarity and nostalgia. There was no doubt about it, in the musical sphere at least Andrew could be very creative, although he never actually played anything. As he got to know me better he grew more spontaneous. My being a clergyman didn't seem to inhibit him, at least not after the first session. Later on he said he was surprised to find himself 'getting on with a vicar'; 'I shouldn't have thought a vicar would have bothered with anyone like me.' I said something self-conscious about vicars being specifically for getting on with people, the gospel being about that sort of thing. It shows how far he had progressed in loosening that Andrew was able to receive this piece of news in a totally unembarrassed way. He simply grinned and went on talking about clergymen he had known.

I think it was the beginning of the tightening process. My interest and rapport – my friendship – was taken as validation of him as a person. It was a few weeks after this that Andrew played a piece right through. It was a Scriabin prelude and he played it right through for me. Or rather, he played it through for both of us. For the relationship.

Wendy was referred to me by her vicar. She was a keen churchgoer, and had organized the Sunday School all her adult life. She was having psychiatric treatment as an out-patient 'but I thought it would be a good idea for her to see you as well because she's such a wonderful church person,' said her vicar. I had a word with Wendy's consultant and she readily gave her consent – 'You'll find her a staunch believer.'

Staunch was the last word I would have used about Wendy. She seemed entirely too volatile. Her moods came and went rapidly, often changing within the length of a single sentence. Happy or sad, she chattered away regardless: her husband, her mother, the children, the neighbours, the news, the children in her Sunday School class, the parish clergy, anything and everything. Thinking that if I managed to get her to stick to the point for long enough I might discover some of the ways in which her world was organized, I got her to produce a self-characterization. Would she write down an account of herself saying who she was and what kinds of things she liked to do? What was important for her and why was it important? Wendy stopped short in the middle of a sentence, looked at the paper I was holding out to her and began to write. After a few minutes she handed the paper back. I saw that she had written out the Nicene Creed, from 'I believe in one God' all the way through to 'the life everlasting'. She sat looking at me with a peculiar look on her face, as if the effort of writing had finally proved cathartic. Without saying anything at all, her attitude was one of triumphant satisfaction. 'Shall we talk about what you've written,' I said. 'No,' she said, 'nothing more to be said.'

In a sense, I knew what she meant. So far as faith goes, after the Creed there's little to be said. As an exercise in self-report, however, it seemed, and still seems, inadequate. I wanted to know more about the woman apart from her identity as someone who accepted certain particular religious propositions. Wendy, however, wasn't going to say any more. I had asked her to reveal herself and she had done so. It was up to me to make what I could of it. In the meantime I was anxious in case I started the chattering off once more.

It was some time before I saw Wendy again. We had agreed that she should come along the week after, but she rang up and postponed the appointment, saying that she didn't really need to come, 'because I'm feeling really well now'. She thanked me for all I had done (*sic*) and rang off; a few days later her vicar told me she had been taken into hospital for treatment. Her behaviour in church had alarmed the congregation so much that her husband had phoned the doctor, with the result that Wendy was now detained for forty-eight hours. The same day I visited her in hospital. Wendy was quiet and serious and explained that she was sure that God had a special purpose for her. The trouble was that she wasn't sure what this was. It existed, however, and it was hers. She said she found it overwhelming – 'I'm driven this way and that, always remembering things, finding new things. There's too much of it for one person, don't you see?' I said I saw all right, I was in the same line of business after all. We would see what we could do. Would she be willing to come along and see me on a regular basis for a few weeks – say, ten – and we would have a go at straightening some things out?

Wendy came to see me, and we set about giving a bit more shape to her chaotic religious awareness. Wendy hid her religious faith behind a mass of detail. When asked to be specific about it, about what she actually believed, she felt constrained to 'get everything in', hence her recitation of the Creed. This had been particularly painful to write down, simply because it was so succinct and definite. Wendy's ideas about religion were uni-polar: in other words she concentrated on the positive poles of her ideas without defining what their negative or 'submerged' poles were. Unfortunately, the negative defines the positive, and vice versa; hers was a religion where ideas were ill-defined because of their lack of contrast. Once I had realized this, the way forward became clearer. We worked together on the central constructs of Christianity, limiting them to the Incarnation, the Redemption, the gift of the Holy Spirit, and the ideas and feelings associated with them. When we considered love, acceptance, self-giving, redemption, expectation, sanctification, etc, we considered their opposites too: that is, the opposites that

Wendy supplied, sometimes with considerable difficulty. Practice in thinking about the 'submerged constructs' of her faith made the whole thing more real for Wendy; as she said, 'Now I feel I know how much I really owe to Jesus.' In this way she could actually think of things which were previously beyond her range. A vague, though important, religious awareness began to assume its proper significance as a system of core constructs able to give purpose and definition to her personal world.

7

Deliverance

Thus says Yahweh,
who made a way through the sea,
a path in great waters;
No need to recall the past
no need to think about what was done before.
See, I am doing a new deed
                                    (Isa. 43.16, 18, 19).

I shall be moving on, in this chapter, to look at aspects of
mental health ministry that are specifically religious. This is
not to say that the approaches we have been considering up
to now are not religious, but that they are not always or not
completely identified with religion. For instance, the comments I have made about our position alongside other professionals reflect a Christian viewpoint but certainly do not
depend on one, owing as much to psychology as theology –
or rather to that area of human awareness in which disciplines
are constantly being cross-referenced, the shared ground of
theology, psychology and sociology. The same is true of the
chapters on counselling and psychotherapy. They are religious
because they were written by somebody – myself – whose
world-view is Christian and whose doctrine of humankind is
basically theological. However, I believe that we need more
than this in order to do our job properly.

  To put this another way, more is needed in the pastoral care
of mentally ill people than understanding and reassurance.

More even than personal validation, although that is the most precious human gift of all. What is needed is the awareness of divine intervention in human affairs for the purpose of renewal and reconstruction. Much is done by personal prayer and intercession, particularly within the framework of worship. The shape of ritual, the shape of a perfect event, brings perfection right into the middle of our human disturbances; men and women who find solitary prayer difficult or even impossible are made aware in corporate ritual of the presence of God and the amazing possibility of change.

This is particularly striking within the sphere of healing. One way or another, most ministers are interested in spiritual healing. You may actually be involved in healing services yourself. It is a controversial subject among clergy, although many more of them regard such services as a legitimate part of the church than did, say, twenty-five years ago. As with psychotherapy, however, I have to say that the heart of ministry to the mentally ill and handicapped does not lie here. If psychotherapy is too scientific, spiritual healing often appears to be not scientific enough! Having said that, the fact remains that the revival of spiritual healing represents a major crisis of confidence on the part of the Christian church, and one which relates directly to the interface of religion and medicine. It will probably play a larger part as time goes on.

When I first arrived at the hospital where I was whole-time chaplain I was rather tentative with regard to those areas of my work which could be construed as being concerned with healing as apart from worship or religious counselling, or whatever else I was employed to do. I myself always found it hard to make distinctions of this kind, but I expected the hospital, and particularly the medical staff, to be in no doubt whatsoever as to what lay within the religious sphere and what was plainly medical. The medical was always to be respected, because it was a hospital, and the women and men to whom I ministered were, by definition of the authorities who employed me, primarily patients. This being the case, I always asked the consultants if they thought it would be a good idea if so-and-so received confirmation. This happened many times during my first ten years, as more and more members of my congregation felt called to become official members of the church. On no occasion did a consultant attempt to interfere, the inevitable response being something along the lines of 'Certainly – you do what you want.' I remember feeling nonplussed by this. Was my contribution so unimportant that it didn't really matter what I did? Couldn't they imagine religion having a serious role to play, either for good or ill, in the psychiatric care of their patients? Later on, when consultants began to refer people to me because they considered them to have 'religious problems' I realized that the reason for their attitude might be rather different; and when I received a good deal of positive support for some research I was carrying out which had a directly psychiatric application, I began to see that I had been quite wrong in my original assessment of the situation.

The fact was that, within certain limitations, the psychiatrists were on the lookout for any help they could get. The younger ones who started arriving at the hospital during the latter half of my service there were certainly much more open to new ideas, including some that were not strictly speaking medical ones, than their predecessors had been. There has been a much greater interchange of ideas and attitudes recently than before. For instance, I had always imagined that it would be seen as an inflammatory act for the chaplain to hold healing services in the hospital church. The medical staff would almost certainly interpret it as some kind of comment on their own efforts to heal people. As for the nurses, there was no telling what their reaction would be. On the whole, however, it was not likely to be favourable: nurses prefer things to be in their proper places, medicine and nursing here, religion definitely there. Even in my last ten years at the hospital it still seemed wiser to effect some kind of compromise. Our patients attended the healing services held in the general hospital chapel next door. Nowadays I would not feel it necessary to be so timid. There is no reason why spiritual healing should not take its place alongside more scientific approaches, every reason why it should. Patients from the psychiatric hospital were greatly helped by attending the healing services. Although I don't remember anybody reporting the total banishment of all psychiatric symptoms, people were refreshed and renewed by the experience, and no one was harmed by it.

I am not surprised that this kind of service, with its authoritative command, 'In the name of Christ, be healed', constitutes a powerful validation of personal worth, the one thing above all that psychiatric patients often feel themselves to be totally lacking in. I recommend services like this, which are factual representations of illness and requests for healing, to priests and ministers, leaving it to their discretion as to whether they think particular people in their charge will benefit from this approach. Most of them will. Two kinds of people need careful support in situations like this: those suffering from paranoid schizophrenia who have delusions which might easily be confirmed; and people with hysterical conditions who may show a rapid, even dramatic, improvement which is short-lived and obviously leads to disappointment and even disillusionment. In my own experience, even these people are not really harmed by healing services, because paranoia tends to interpret everything, 'religious' or not, as confirmation of itself, and hysterics may be warned that their violent experience of deliverance, even though it may not last, constitutes a message of God's love which should not be undervalued.

My own experience with people who were 'hearing voices' led me to believe that people who suffer from a paranoid psychosis are not immediately affected by the message of loving acceptance and renewal transmitted by the laying on of hands. I suppose I should have known better than to hope they would be, of course. I had read in John Richardson's book *Deliver Us From Evil* that the Ministry of Deliverance is not a form of psychiatric treatment, because people who are spiritually afflicted are not necessarily mentally ill. Exorcism, in other words, is not a way of removing psychiatric symptoms. Nevertheless, on two occasions, in a desperate bid to help but against my better judgment, I used the formulae for exorcism. The first patient was still hearing voices when I saw her the next day: 'Never mind,' she said. 'I didn't think anything would shift them. It was a good try.' The second patient's voices told him how worthless he was – only fit to do away with himself. This young man is very much better now, thank God, so the exorcism may have had an effect. At the time and for months afterwards, he felt no better at all.

According to Richardson and the authorities he cites, spiritual possession affects the conscious will rather than the functions of cognition and emotion distorted by psychiatric illness. People who are possessed are remarkably clear-minded in every other direction. They give few indications of a personality which has lost touch with its environment of people and things. Almost always are they religious people, usually church members. Somewhere in their lives, however, there is a secret, something too painful to be contemplated. It is this fact that causes them to be 'haunted' or 'possessed'. From a psychiatric point of view such a person would be considered to be hysteric. Hysteria is a neurotic reaction to experiences which are too painful to be thought about, but find expression in other forms, as physical symptoms or, in this case, sensory illusions. Christians have drawn attention to episodes in human life which have caused endemic spiritual disturbances, unfinished business which has been ignored or covered over and demands satisfaction. The two explanations of the 'possession syndrome', psychiatric and theological, are remarkably similar, the first being a demythologized version of the second. This makes it possible for priest and psychatrist to work together to a certain extent. Again, it is not advisable to 'go it alone', even with the support of the diocesan authorities. This is a case for the very closest co-operation with the psychiatrist.

Molly's twin sister was a student nurse at a famous teaching hospital. She had two elder sisters, both of them career women in well-paid jobs. Her only brother, a little boy of ten, had died a year before I met her. This was roughly five years after the father of the family had run away from home with another woman. Everybody said that Molly's mother, Mrs Stevens, was a marvellous woman to have brought up five children on her own. Her vicar spoke very highly of her as being warm and sympathetic, a real friend to her daughters, and when I met her myself I got the same impression. She was a faithful churchwoman and this had helped her during the difficult times associated with Mr Stevens' desertion and Richard's death. Even now the family troubles were not over. Several times during the last few years Molly's behaviour had made the rest of the family ashamed of her. On two occasions she had been brought into the psychiatric hospital after taking overdoses of tablets. It wasn't as if she was really ill, in which case the family would have been only too glad to have been sorry for her. The psychiatrist, Dr Glover, described the difficulty to Mrs Stevens as 'personality disorder'. 'I could have told him that,' Mrs Stevens said.

I first came into contact with Molly when her vicar came to see me. Her vicar, not her mother's. Molly had chosen her own congregation to belong to. She was very keen on church, and often went to her mother's on Sunday mornings, taking in her own in the evening. I think a powerful factor here was her liking for clergymen, whom she treated as substitute fathers. She certainly attached herself to me with the greatest determination, following me everywhere I went around the hospital until I had to ask her firmly to desist. ('Why? You think people think we're 'aving it off?') Molly was having bad dreams, in which her brother Richard spoke to her and urged her to kill herself so that they could be together as they used to be. She had also tried to contact Richard himself with an ouija board and received frightening messages from that too. Finally, she came to see me in my office and asked if it would be possible for her to be exorcised.

In the hour that followed Molly told me things which, she said, she had never told anyone before. She certainly spoke quite differently. Instead of her usual loud comments and brash mode of delivery, she spoke slowly and carefully, as if she found difficulty in getting the words out. Several times she broke down; and when she finished it was because she was crying too much to talk any more.

She told me how she and Richard had been in the habit of breaking into buildings and stealing what they could find there. She wouldn't have told me this, it was none of my business, she said, but she wanted to speak to me about Richard. It was to do with the way they worked – she broke the windows and Richard climbed through and opened up for her. The system worked well usually. This time, however, they had decided to break into Richard's school. Over confident, he had climbed in by himself and had fallen through the skylight and broken his neck. Molly came round shortly after and found him lying amid all the broken glass. Instead of sending for the police, she ran off as fast as she could, leaving him by himself.

'I thought he was dead. I'm sure he was dead. Now he wants me with him! What can I do, Roger?'

With Molly's permission I consulted her vicar, her mother's vicar, my own clerical colleague, and Molly's friend the Youth Chaplain. We resolved to try the Ministry of Deliverance, if this was acceptable to Dr Glover. I was deputed to put the case to him. 'Surely you don't believe that kind of magic?' he said. 'Whether I do or not,' I replied, 'Molly does. Perhaps we should try speaking to her in her own language.' Dr Glover agreed that I had a point. Could the service proceed? Certainly, if I thought that it would do any good!

To be honest, I wasn't at all sure that I did 'believe'. I hadn't done anything like this before. What I had read about it seemed convincing but actually doing it was different. As it turned out I was glad that my uncertainty didn't communicate itself to Dr Glover and that somehow I had managed to find exactly the right formula for getting through to him.

The exorcism was arranged for a fortnight later, to take place in the hospital chapel. Molly was calmer now than I had ever known her to be. I hardly spoke to her at all during the intervening period. She obviously needed to be by herself. Whether she was frightened, I don't know, and I didn't ask her. The exorcist was a local vicar, a man of authoritative personality (he had been a colonel in the army). However, it was not his personality but Christ's that banished whatever evil there was in that chapel. The service went on for an hour and a half. I shall never forget it. I was exhausted and so were my colleagues. I wondered how Molly must be feeling. At last it was over. Molly tottered over to the chapel door. She hadn't said a word throughout the exorcism. Now she turned a radiant smile on us. 'For God's sake give us a fag,' she said.

Not everyone will want to work in this area. Some people may consider themselves to be temperamentally unfitted to do so. I myself would think more than twice before making it my main sphere of work. I was more or less dragged into it by the particular circumstances of Molly's case, which seemed to indicate the Ministry of Deliverance very clearly; and not only to me but to several other clergy. Even so, when it came to it, we did not attempt to do it ourselves but preferred to call in a specialist, a priest of many years' experience in this particular field. On the whole it was a considerable emotional strain for all of us, not least those who had been most sceptical. (One of us was was heard to say that he 'wouldn't have been surprised to see something with horns and a tail emerge' – a strange thing for someone with a degree in science to say!) Molly wasn't the only one who was relieved when it was over.

But it was over. Richard had gone home for good. Whether

one explains this psychoanalytically or spiritually, Molly was 'cured'. Freud maintains that the 'possession syndrome' occurs only in immature people, relating specifically to those suffering from paternal deprivation. In this state there is an irresistible urge for power to be exercised both over and on behalf of the individual, and demonism of one form or another offers a substitute for legitimate authority. Certainly Molly surrounded herself with father figures, on whose time and attention she made excessive demands. She could never get enough, in fact. The ouija board may well have opened up a new, more exciting avenue for self-magnification. The fact that she herself certainly never looked at things in this way doesn't make the idea any less credible. After all, we are dealing here with motives and desires that are unconscious.

Whether or not this is the case – or a valid way of looking at the case – the fact remains that it was the service of exorcism that was the occasion of the cure, and the priest rather than the psychiatrist who, using 'power from elsewhere', actually brought it about. Ritual is the sphere of the embodied Spirit, a form of action carried out by women and men as the expression of their specifically religious identity. Whatever one may feel about the Ministry of Deliverance as such, there is a sense in which all our services are ministries of deliverance, particularly the sacramental ones; and even the non-sacramental ones that we offer in the intention of loving intercession.

The service of exorcism described here is just about the most dramatic example of a church service I could find, the least like the things that go on in ordinary life. In this happening, religion stood out in very high relief. It worked and was seen to work. The important thing, however, is to recognize the fact that other rituals and celebrations of Christian belief also 'work', and that they do so in the same unambiguous way, by declaring the active presence of faith in Christ. Whether the worship is led by a Roman Catholic or a member of the Society of Friends, the action he or she leads is the performance of an identifiable role as a minister of the gospel, a role which is successfully performed to the extent that it is *identifiable* either by a person or a group of people. There are other things that we do, but the worship of God, *performed as a different kind of activity*, is the most important of all.

When I was a chaplain I found that the effect of informal services should not be overestimated. These were the occasions that drew attention to themselves by taking care not to do so. Silent groups of people holding hands convey just as much, if not more, of a blessing than noisy hymn singing. I used to think that our small al fresco eucharists must be kept well out of the public gaze in case other people felt excluded, accusing us of considering ourselves to be superior. I certainly didn't want to make alienated people feel even worse. One day, however, the Registrar on an Acute Ward came up and thanked us for holding a service 'where I can hear it going on'. This was to happen quite frequently in the years ahead. I think that of all the things about psychiatric chaplaincy I enjoyed, this meant the most to me. I am sure that this sort of area, concerned with the healing power of ritual, invites development. It draws attention to the true nature of our role, which is not to be a religious psychotherapist but a woman or man of God.

Having said that, ministers and priests of all kinds need to be able to work in a variety of spheres and roles, with individuals as well as groups, using all the information they can get, not all of which will be theological although it may certainly be interpreted theologically. There is truth for a Christian minister in everything that other disciplines know about people, so long as it is genuine knowledge and not a reduction of humanness. Where such reduction takes place, theological understanding can still recognize the value of the original truth which has become distorted by the need to control things which elude understanding, facts whose meaning lies precisely in their elusiveness. Cliché though it may be, we need to develop the skill in looking at life through theological eyes, so that all our work, whether it concerns mentally ill, mentally handicapped or so-called normal people contributes to our specific mission, which is to minister to everybody in the name of Christ and on behalf of his church. There is a lot of difference between Molly's service, the shortened mass held in the group home sitting room, and choral evensong in the parish church; but they are all services of healing in that they reveal the distinctive nature of the church in a way that only worship can do.

8

The Most Important Thing

The most important thing about mentally ill and mentally handicapped people is, in fact, that they *are* people. In other words, working with mentally handicapped and mentally ill people brings home the reality of our common humanity. I don't think I can bring this home powerfully enough. These people are ourselves, bone of our bone, flesh of our flesh, blood of our blood. They are neither their illness nor their handicap. We not only do them an injustice when we treat them as though their interest lies in their difference from ourselves, we deprive ourselves of the life of mutuality which could exist between us if we would allow it to do so. A book about ministry to the mentally ill and mentally handicapped may easily do as much harm as good to its subjects, because it encourages us to adopt a kind of pseudo-scientific attitude towards them, which deprives them of their humanity.

I believe that the personhood of men and women triumphs over any of the things that can happen to them that affect their personalities; certainly over factors concerning their intellectual development. There is always a tendency to regard anything that causes temporary or permanent dependence as if it involves regression to an infantile condition: 'Does he take sugar?' Disabled people easily feel depersonalized. Those who can't walk, for instance, complain that they are treated like wheel-chairs, not people. Because of the frightening ideas about total irrationality surrounding mental illness and mental handicap, this can grow out of all proportion until those concerned are never spoken to – or of – as people at all.

Never addressed as themselves even by those trained and paid to help them, who always see them in terms of their psychiatric symptoms, or let those symptoms cloud their impression of them as people. Never addressed as themselves by their families, who, whilst admitting that it could happen to anybody, would rather not acknowledge that it has actually happened to a person in their family.

It is very easy for us as clergy to adopt either of these approaches. Both the 'family' attitude and the 'professional' one come easy to us; besides, we need to start somewhere, and the area may be one that we regard as out of our sphere. In fact, I don't think we can avoid treating patients and ex-patients like this to begin with. It is only as we get to know them that we begin to meet them, neither as 'social rejects' nor 'mental cases' but as themselves, strangers to be met who become people to be known and loved.

After all, the only way to know them is as people, individuals with whom you share your humanity and exchange your experience. When you begin to do this, what is shared begins to take precedence over whatever is strange, until the person that emerges has ceased to be simply an example of illness or handicap and can be regarded as someone like you, perhaps even someone you admire, with characteristics you would like to possess. When that happens then you can turn your attention to the things that constitute illness or handicap and see them as problems that a person has, not as the actual identity of that person. You can work with the person and learn from them. Because you are neither a psychiatrist nor a family member you are in a privileged position. He or she is someone you are in a position to get to know personally.

This is a kind of knowledge that doesn't ignore disability, but sees it in perspective, as something that affects personality without being the person themselves. My experience in a psychiatric hospital brought home to me the fact that people are bigger than the psychiatric signs and symptoms, whether of handicap of illness. At first I was inhibited by other people's assessments, admiring the professionalism of those who saw patients as typical examples of one or other kinds of disability. Then I got to know the people concerned and my attitude gradually changed.

Jimmy and I used to wander along by the perimeter fence, talking about railways. Jimmy had been an engine driver on the 'Lanky', the old Lancashire and Yorkshire Railway. Like many clergy, I have always been fascinated by steam railways, but I hadn't known many actual drivers so Jimmy's stories filled me with delight. Here at last was someone who was able to explain how the valve gear worked. 'Course I will,' he said. 'We'll need some paper. I'll go back and get some.' And away he started across the playing fields towards the wing of the hospital he was living in. I walked back beside him. When he reached his ward the Charge Nurse beckoned me to one side and asked me politely if Jimmy talked to me. I said that he did, quite a lot and quite often. 'That's interesting,' said the Charge Nurse. 'He never says a word when he's on the ward.' I asked him how long Jimmy had been in the hospital. I said that Jimmy had told me twenty-seven years. 'Oh, he said that did he? I shouldn't pay much attention to him. He's schizophrenic, you know.' Jimmy hobbled into the office and stood waiting for his tablets. I looked at him again. He looked quite different. I said, 'All right, Jimmy?' He grinned and shuffled away.

As I suggested early on in this book, our task with regard to mental illness or handicap is one of communication. This was so when men and women were incarcerated within psychiatric hospitals; it is equally so today. People like Jimmy carry a hospital around with them, even when they leave. As I said, to be saddled with a psychiatric diagnosis is to be incarcerated within a social stereotype, to wear it in public like a scuba diver's wet suit, the compulsory exoskeleton of your official self. It is to carry someone around who isn't you at all but within whom you aren't allowed to be anyone. In hospital, for the sake of a quiet life, you obediently played the role of patient. Outside you find yourself as stuck with it as you were inside. Because of your problems you are only permitted to exist in a reduced guise, as someone who is inferior almost by definition, someone people are expected to regard with at least pity, at worse contempt. You are frightened by these people who have such power over you, and they are frightened of you. In a very real sense you are homeless. When the people around you resent your presence how can you really call it 'home'? 'I'll tell you it sticks, having been in there; it sticks like shit,' Rosie said in a discussion at the MIND drop-in centre.

Wherever ex-patients meet, the problem is discussed. The discussion never really gets anywhere in the sense of reaching conclusions as to what should be done, what practical steps should be taken. It simply serves as a way of letting off steam. The real work of bridging the gap goes on elsewhere, in situations involving both sides, formal and informal: council meetings in which decisions are taken regarding the locations of group homes for mentally handicapped people, incidents in supermarkets and on the streets of council estates where the two sides come into contact and the need for mutual understanding and acceptance is felt by both. Clergy play a crucial role in such encounters, because they are often called in to adjudicate and end up acting as interpreters for both sides. This is the kind of job they are used to doing, after all. As ministers of reconciliation, the overall aim is to be a harmonizing presence, someone more concerned with people than processes, relationships than techniques. Someone who sets out to be a person rather than a professional. They look askance at those of their number who appear to be seeking some kind of technical validation by knowing too much about psychotherapy.

However, as an 'outsider' your exposed position and absence of any recognizable technical skill inevitably suggest that you be cast in a communications role, moving freely from

person to person. This is your function as a carer; at best a
valuable facilitation of the work of the professionals, at worst
a clumsy cleric getting in everyone's way. You may think that
this is undignified and unstable. Perhaps, but it is the more or
less inevitable fate of the lone clergy person on his or her
dealings with inter-professional organizations. This kind of
set-up can rapidly become a struggle for power as different
professions strive to reach a commanding position within the
institutional network. Your aim will be to assist in main-
taining the balance that is essential if things are to go the way
they should for the benefit of those you are trying to help –
co-operatively rather then competitively.

Here are some ways in which clergy can hold the balance
in mental health.

1. They can ask to be invited to join various committees
concerned with health matters. Many, if not most, people
who are members of hospitals and community committees
consider the clergy to be more or less harmless (no time to go
into this here!) and will not attach very much significance to
your presence. This is a wonderful opportunity to sit back
with your ears and eyes open. It is important to ask, because
nobody will think of inviting you otherwise. This is because
they don't think you will be interested. You will find that,
more often than not, your fellow professionals from other
disciplines actually value your presence. So long as you find
ways of being really useful, your colleagues will interpret your
function in ways that permit you to involve yourself in all
sorts of areas. Only you can discover what these are – they
will be different for each person. Some discretion is needed,
to make sure that you are not trespassing in areas definitely
attached to someone else's field of official responsibility. To
do this is to leave yourself open to the justified annoyance of
people who are paid to do a particular job and don't welcome
interference from over-eager clergymen. So far as support
roles go, however, there are few limitations to your usefulness;
and there are often things to be done which no one else has

been deputed to concern themselves with. Altogether it is surprising how often, and in how many areas, the clergy's involvement is appreciated and not simply tolerated. It is up to you to find these out for yourself, but my advice would always be – don't be too timid. You might be just the person they are looking for, but you will almost always have to ask, and perhaps point out the relevance of what you have to offer both as a person and as clergymen.

2. This is all connected with your general attitude to mental health professionals. Obviously, with them, medical and nursing concerns will always tend to take priority. There's nothing personal about it: but there will be if you try to throw your weight around. If you keep a reasonably low profile in the demands you make for assistance and/or co-operation you will find you have every opportunity to get as involved as you want – or have time – to be.

3. Apart from the professionals there are amateurs, particularly those working within a professional setting. The Community Health Council exists to act as a watchdog to the statutory health service in a particular area. It consists of men and women who represent the various bodies and agencies making up the public life of the area, both statutory and non-statutory. Almost everybody, in one way or another, from the Town Hall to the Deanery Synod, has a representative on the CHC! Whereas its work hardly affected hospital chaplains in the past, work within the community now requires close co-operation with this body, particularly with regard to attitudes towards the provision for mental illness.

4. The connection with MIND is more obvious. This, too, owes its origin to government legislation, but functions in an entirely different way by means of semi-independent local associations. The local Association for Mental Health usually needs all the help it can get in the way of involvement and expertise and, particularly, money. Because it receives no funds from either the health authority or the social services – or anywhere else – it depends entirely on fund-raising events

and flag days. Because mental health is far from being a public priority (because it reminds people of mental *illness*, a subject they prefer to forget), many associations live a hand-to-mouth existence. What resources they do manage to gather together are spent directly on helping ex-patients. They set up drop-in centres and provide first-hand support at times when help is not forthcoming. Originally established to encourage awareness on the part of the community of the possibility that the mentally ill could be helped without banishment to huge psychiatric hospitals, MIND is now struggling to come to terms with a situation in which the hospital population has been summarily evicted from its homes and expected to merge indistinguishably with the host community. Mental health chaplains should not need to work hard to establish a relationship with their local mental health associations. It exists already. It only needs following up and encouraging.

5. What about your fellow Christians? Anglicans will belong to the Deanery Chapter and the Deanery Synod, perhaps to the Diocesan Synod as well, and ministers of other denominations have their corresponding networks or ways in which they belong to their own particular church systems. Apart from the institutional links, however, a priest or minister working in the community has strong personal ties with the surrounding congregations and their clergy. I think that it is at this level and on these terms that the battle against stigma must be fought. I shall say more about this later on; though it is worth pointing out here that anyone working in this field will spend a good deal of time preaching and talking to church groups about mental health, and perhaps writing about it as well. The Anglican Diocesan Director of Social Responsibility, and his or her counterpart in other denominations are available to give advice in this area. Relationships with the Social Services are crucial!

6. Much of the hard work done by health authorities and mental health teams nowadays takes place in the area of rehabilitation. This can be a crucial area for the church

because it represents the changeover from life in the institution to life within the community. As the large mental hospitals close down, more and more effort is devoted to trying to help patients who are used to living in the special, protected environment that they provide adjust to life within the community. 'Rehab' is no longer simply a matter of making sure that an ex-patient is as well – that is, as free from symptoms – as possible before being discharged; the aim nowadays is to ally each person with an environment which he or she will find congenial, one that they will want to leave hospital *for*. To do this the department needs help, both inside and outside hospital. The clergy are obviously key people; they and their congregations provide ready-made social groups to which ex-patients can relate, whether or not they are churchgoers themselves. The rehab department is an important link for congregations seeking to help the mentally ill and handicapped. Again, you will almost certainly have to make the first move here as well. The practicability of congregational membership isn't always obvious to those in other disciplines!

7. From April 1993 local authority care of psychiatric patients in the community will be in the hands of social work departments. The churches already have links with these through their own 'departments of social responsibility'. There is an opportunity here for increased contact and better understanding.

In all this, you and your congregation are breaking new ground. Almost certainly you will have no established procedures to guide you. You will have to make your own 'space' in terms of working relations, and prove your usefulness in terms of others' appreciation of your work. A lot of the time you will seem like an intruder, and the probability is that you will feel, from time to time, very isolated. It takes a lot of courage to break ground as new as this.

Important though this balancing act is, it is secondary to another task which co-operatively rather than competitively confronts clergy in their care for mentally ill and emotionally disabled people – that of helping their own congregations to become more aware of their needs and less frightened of their presence. Basically this involves passing on the enthusiasm that you yourself have, in as immediate and personal a way as you can. This can be done by inviting someone to speak to the congregation about mentally disturbed and mentally handicapped people, and the problems that they have. This is better than inviting speakers for particular groups within the church, as this suggests that the subject can be seen as a group interest rather than a matter of general concern. It would also be better to separate the two areas of mental illness and mental handicap which so often become confused. Both MIND and APCMI are willing to supply speakers, and the local Mental Health Chaplain will be only too glad to come along.

The help of the Mental Health Chaplain is available to all clergy in his or her area as a resource person for the welfare of mentally ill or handicapped people. They co-operate with the local clergy in doing this, visiting them at home and making contact with them at the places where they gather together around the town, particularly the day centres and drop-in centres. Most of the mental health chaplains I know prefer a one-to-one approach or like to meet people in small groups. Some of their most productive work is done as facilitators of interest in mental health within congregations – not simply talking to the people, but encouraging them to work among themselves towards a greater understanding, a deeper acceptance. I have said that if the ill and the handicapped are to be known as the precious individuals that they are, they must not simply be acknowledged and respected (respect is so easily confused with rejection) but actively taken to the heart of the congregation. This is the only way in which they will be known.

This takes more than a handshake and a cup of coffee; more than remembering someone's name and making sure that they are visited at home; even more than giving them a job to do in the congregation. It takes determination on both sides, to know someone and to love them. It takes time for an entire culture to be unlearned. It takes Holy Spirit.

Some of the people moving into our congregations carry this with them. Bert used to live on Crofton Ward. (It was pointed out to me a few days ago by a patient that people are accommodated *on* psychiatric wards but *in* general wards. I hadn't thought of this myself, but it seems to be the case. It implies a kind of institutional impersonality which may, in fact, be totally misleading.) Bert has only been on this ward for a few months, but he has lived in the hospital for twenty-five years, having spent twenty years in another psychiatric hospital before coming here. As far as Bert is concerned he has always been on the move. His life in the two hospitals has been a succession of minor upheavals reflecting alterations in official policy, the continual process of ward improvement or re-decoration, the process of ward closure and consequent redeployment of patients. In ordinary human terms this means that men and women who have lived in a particular place long enough for it to become personal to them, and have made friends they can really trust, undergo an experience as a result of which they are deprived of both. This may not seem to be a very great hardship for those who never chose to come here in the first place, and who loathe the hospital and themselves for being in it. (Patients like this – and there are many of them – grow attached to their own personal environment of bed-space, shelf-unit, armchair, and object strongly to having to exchange it for one that really belongs to someone else ... Even if your world consists of the particular corner of the dayroom where nurse sets you down on your bean-bag, you feel angry when it is suddenly a different corner in an alien room. I have been on wards which have just been resettled in this way and felt the anger which hovers in the atmosphere, and not only among the patients.)

Bert, however, is different. Apart from the traumatic event of becoming a patient at his first hospital, and the changes involved in leaving there and being transferred to this one, Bert has been forced to decamp dozens of times during the quarter century he has been here. To him, however, each move is a challenge and an adventure. He is not simply used to changing wards – indeed, it usually seems to come as a surprise to him, a welcome surprise because of the new opportunities it presents. For Bert each disruption of routine is a promise of a new lease of life, a time and place to glorify God. For Bert, ward exchanges are staging posts on the journey to broader acres.

His spiritual journey began sixty or so years ago in a town about ten miles away from the hospital. He belonged to a churchgoing family and attended first Sunday School, then choir, gaining a knowledge of the prayer book and psalter which has been with him ever since. (He mourns the day they gave up saying Matins in the hospital church.) His brother was already working down the pit, and as soon as he was old enough Bert, too, became a collier. He does not seem to have objected to this; in that place, at that time, there was little else to do in the way of work. Bert has a cheerful disposition and makes his experiences sound quite exciting. It was dark there in the pit, though, and he didn't like that: 'It was just black. It must've been a whole mile under the earth.' Perhaps it was the blackness that defeated him; the contrast between the coal dust on his hands and the visionary brilliance within his mind that led him to opt for the latter to the extent of denying his former existence.

Anyway, Bert did not last long down the mine. Instead he went mad and was admitted to the first of his two psychiatric hospitals. I do not know the precise diagnosis, but the main symptom must have been joy. Bert's life is characterized by the tendency to see hope in every direction, coupled, it must be said, by a grasp of the facts which is not always as reliable as it might be. Both these tendencies are considered to be signs of insanity, the joy giving rise to more institutional discomposure than the disordered thought ever did. Three quarters of the time he is speaking to you Bert makes perfect sense: then because he sees a connection you do not, or chooses to ignore a logical rule most people regard as essential, you have a powerful sense of having lost the thread somewhere and want to ask if you can start again and get it right this time. Conversations of this kind are usually considered to be of clinical interest only, the way in which something is said being more important than what is actually meant. Not being a psychiatrist I have always been interested in the message rather than the diagnosis; and Bert's messages are usually very important indeed. This is what he has to say on the subject of illness and God, a crucial one for human life in general and hospitals in particular: 'You love one person who makes you better. Nurses, doctors. It's like God. If God lets you get poorly and you love him he makes you better. God makes you better.' This seems straightforward enough, although one does not often hear it said quite like that. What is strange, however, is Bert's attitude to the immediate reality of God. He makes it sound as if God were present in just the same way as anybody else, not as a theological assumption but as a plain ordinary fact. He cannot see God: but then he doesn't need to, because 'It's all God, everything's God, you know'; he certainly does not confuse himself, as an individual, with God, as people suffering from schizophrenia are sometimes supposed to do. God is Bert's fellow traveller, around the hospital and through life. The lack of structure in Bert's thinking gives his awareness of God an awe-inspiring flexibility and comprehensiveness. Technically of course he is more of a poet than a theologian, but the same could be said of Henry Vaughan, Thomas Traherne, or even St John of the Cross. Bert has none of their expressive skill. What he says is notable for its meaning rather than its form. His language is blunt, ramming home the splendid obviousness of the transcendent. Most people on first meeting him find him rather ridiculous and want to know why he is so happy. Poor thing, to be happy in a place like this! Surely that proves he must be ill! It's not normal to be grinning all the time!

Bert's not always grinning, however. He certainly tends to grin a lot when he is talking to people, but this is because people give him great joy. When he is walking through the hospital grounds alone he looks quite solemn. Not sad, just calmly reflective. I used to wonder what he was thinking about. Something profoundly unsubtle and totally memorable, the kind of corny vision of total glory that we have categorized out of existence.

Bert's eyes are fixed on the distant hills, and the landscape through which he passes reflects their glory. Madge sits in the garden and looks back to the past. The past is very real to Madge, very real and very necessary, for it gives her spiritual strength to bear the burdens of the present and deal with her fears about the future. Many people in the hospital look back with longing to the days before they were admitted. It seems to them that they used to live in a totally different world from the one they now inhabit. A patient on an acute admission ward lies in bed at night, hands over ears to keep out the hospital sounds, and imagines it is his or her own bed at home. Near the hospital greenhouses an elderly gentleman stubs out a cigarette and aches to have a trowel in his hands again: his own trowel, in his own earth. Many of the patients of Madge's generation – she is seventy-five – have completely lost touch with their families, some because their relatives have died or can no longer be traced, others because the people in question simply wanted it to be so. They intended the split to be permanent and did not want to be involved any longer with the sick person. Everything had been carried out properly. The hospital was the best place; after all, it was what it was for. For the good of all concerned, he or she had finally been 'put away'. We may imagine that in a case like this a patient's thoughts of home might be characterized by a degree of resentment. As month gives way to month, year to year, decade to decade, the image of home is likely to be distorted. There is no living link between past and present, only a vague and shifting impression of love and security which somehow went horribly wrong, leaving its legacy of ingrained resentment and a sense of having been betrayed.

Madge has been spared such feelings, thank God. Her time in hospital has been unshadowed by any kind of emotional turmoil apart from the usual annoyances and small jealousies of institutional life. Her history is reflected on her face, which is smooth and unwrinkled, a characteristic of people who have lived in sheltered circumstances and avoided the wear and tear of a sink or swim society. In fact, she has always lived in institutions, having been brought up in an orphanage run by Dr Barnardo's. In a way this is the most important thing about Madge; or at least, it is what she herself considers to be most important. Even now, sixty years after she moved into her first job, her life is built around the orphanage which was her first home. She sits on the tiny lawn in front of the immense ward-block reading her monthly letter from Barnardo's. If you show any interest at all she will tell you exactly what it says. You get the impression that Madge still believes she is there, at the orphanage, along with all her friends. Two hundred miles and sixty years from the place she loves most, the place that is home, Madge remains a Barnardo's girl.

Her first 'position' was as a housemaid to a doctor's family in the East End. She was very happy there for ten years; then, when she was twenty-six she left to get married. She does not say much about this time in her life. It appears that her husband left her soon after the birth of her first (and only) child. He was a hairdresser's assistant and seems to have left Madge for a more glamorous consort. At this critical point in her life, with a small child to look after, Barnardo's rose to the occasion and took Madge in as a kind of junior house mother. This was another period of happiness; like the first it came to an end, although Madge and Charlie – named after his father – did manage to stay on for several years. They would probably have stayed longer if tragedy had not struck. Playing on a rubbish dump Charlie cut his knee. The wound turned septic, and within a fortnight he was dead. Nowadays, as Madge points out, he could easily have been saved with penicillin.

Madge left Barnardo's for a second time. This time she headed north in the hope of contacting her husband's family. As it turned out it was a vain hope; she couldn't find them, and even if she could have done there was not much chance of their helping her. Her husband had severed all connection with them on first leaving home for London. Madge did not even know if they knew he had got married. With the little boy to show them there might have been some chance ... After a few weeks of scavenging from dustbins and sleeping in doorways she gave up hope of finding them. By this time she was in a wretched state: hungry, dirty and threadbare. Now, some months after Charlie's death, the full force of her loss attacked her and she literally did not know which way to turn. A well-meaning clergyman had her admitted to the mental hospital. This man asked her where she had come from, and when she said Barnardo's he immediately got into contact with the orphanage to enquire what he should do. Did they want him to put Madge on a train and send her back to London? Barnardo's did not feel that they were in any position to take Madge back again, considering the circumstances. She had left of her own free will and might decide to do so again. She was obviously in a disturbed state of mind and needed special treatment that they were not equipped to provide. Besides, they were not at all sure that Madge would want to go home again. Had she been asked? Madge was asked and said that she felt too guilty to return to Barnardo's, and that this place – the asylum – was no more than she deserved. She was admitted on 4 July 1930, diagnosed as suffering from depression.

Ten weeks after her admission Madge wrote to Dr Barnardo's describing her new home and giving short pen pictures of her fellow patients and members of the hospital staff. She didn't think she would be here for long, she said, the people were nice, though not so nice as at Barnardo's, and she was looking forward to seeing her old friends again. It was the first of dozens, even hundreds, of such letters that she wrote during the next fifty-five years, at the rate of one per fortnight with an extra one for Christmas and Easter. The wonderful thing is that her letters were always answered. There was always someone at Barnardo's to write back. Her gift for describing people and events made her letters very amusing and this may be one of the reasons why she always received a reply. The replies were personal, addressed to Miss Madge Brocklebank, Grange Ward, Western Meads Hospital, and written in longhand rather than on a typewriter or in the form of a circular. (I remember that on one occasion she did get a printed letter, one of the fund-raising circulars that charities send out in their thousands. Madge was astonished to read 'Dear Miss Brocklebank' instead of 'Dear Madge'. They never called her that! Who could have written it? She didn't recognize the name at all. They seemed to want her to send them money. It was all very worrying and not a little frightening. I did my best to reassure her, saying that it was a mistake and not really meant for her at all. I don't think she was convinced. It was addressed to Madge Brocklebank and there was no one else at Western Meads called that, was there?

Bert and Madge are just about to leave the hospital to be rehoused in the community, Madge in a group home with three other women, Bert in a block of supervised flats. I have written about them at some length in order to show something of the world they have come from as that world actually is. It seems to me that the most important thing we can do if we want to change peoples' attitudes towards their new neighbours is to overcome the terrible feeling of alienation that characterizes the relationship. We talk a lot about the fear of mental illness, usually explaining it in terms of our natural

bafflement when faced with people we can't understand
because they neither think nor feel the way we do, so that we
have no idea how they will react to our presence. What if they
suddenly take the idea into their heads to become violent? No
one can predict what they might do ... better keep them at a
safe distance. Actually it is the 'safe distance' idea that makes
us so terrified. By alienating them from us we have alienated
ourselves from them, so that we have absolutely no chance of
understanding them and feel driven to keep them perpetually
at arm's length. Aliens are, by definition, people you can't
understand. By alienating these people we have absolved ourselves from needing to find out about them. We say we can't
understand them; what we mean is that we don't want to. If
we did we might have to start feeling differently, behaving
differently. It's as if we are terrified of finding out that they
are people after all ...

This is a great pity, and in some cases a tragedy. Particularly
nowadays. Modern psychiatric treatment is able to reduce the
frighteningly bizarre symptoms that dominate our imagination, so that ex-patients can react to people and things in
what we consider to be the 'right' way. For the first time,
people who know nothing about psychiatric illness can help
those who suffer from it at first hand by befriending them
and, if necessary, reminding them to take the medication
that obviously helps them so much. Having once broken off
relations with mental illness as part of life, albeit a mon-
strously troublesome one, and consigned it to an exclusive
existence outside the camp, it is immensely hard to get it back.
It certainly takes more than a change in government policy.

And yet it is our unwillingness to have them, not theirs to
come. Most of the ex-patients I know are eager to settle down
and lead 'normal' lives in the community. Coming from a
large institution in which social behaviour was invariably
rewarded they are taken aback when people they say 'hello'
to drop their glance, mumble and make off as quickly as
possible. When I speak to groups of people about my job

working with psychiatric patients I tell them about people like Bert and Madge, making sure, of course, that I have properly disguised their identity. By concentrating on people rather than ideas I hope to bring home the living reality of the situation and give my audience a glimpse of it from the other side of the wall. If I can bring the two worlds together in this way then I can access the imagination of my hearers so that they can begin to sense the presence of a fascinating landscape where there use to be only forbidden territory. The difficulty is to find ways of transporting this interest away from the church, school hall or lecture theatre to the streets, living rooms and shopping malls of the town.

Many local churches have found ways of helping former patients by welcoming them into the various associations attached to the church or setting up, perhaps in co-operation with other congregations, special drop-in centres aimed at relieving their boredom and providing the right kind of sympathetic fellowship. Some churches have been more ambitious and have provided counselling services for ex-patients and those receiving treatment within the community. Unless they involve first-hand contact with ex-patients on the part of the congregation itself, these things are in danger of alienating those they set out to help by limiting their social contacts to various specialist activities, and so confirming them in their sense of being 'different'. Again, church people have said to me that they would rather not commit themselves; they have no objection to the newcomers attending church – indeed they will try and make them as welcome as they can – but to undertake more would be to relieve the authorities of a load which is really theirs and so collude with the government's refusal to face its own responsibilities. I must say that I understand this attitude, but it is not my own. It seems to me that the men and women I am concerned for are a forgotten minority, with no political power to speak of, so they can be ignored with impunity. Certainly the lack of concern on the part of the churches is not likely to fill the government with remorse! Apart from which, the churches must respond to a situation like this, at the risk of denying the gospel for whose sake they exist, the particular expression and implementation of God's universal purpose of reconciliation.

Stated baldly this looks very like a truism. The whole church, in Christ, serves the purposes of God. However, I believe that I am right in regarding this kind of service as specially significant. In fact, I believe it to be even more so than any other kind. As human beings we live within the sphere of understanding. We believe that the Word was made flesh to encounter us within our sphere of understanding; for our understanding is the knowing of human beings, an embodiment awareness. This kind of embodied awareness is authentic human understanding, not a disembodied category of 'mind' or 'soul' but a real personal presence, a being towards the other person. This is precisely what mentally disturbed people find so difficult; what, so long as they are ill, they can't do. And so they typify our own estrangement. Perhaps this is why we shut them away or simply hope they will wander off of their own accord: they remind us of ourselves. These mentally disturbed, humanly alienated people are *our* word made flesh. Working alongside them we find ourselves at the epicentre of the gospel.

It is in this sphere of human life, where illness and handicap remind us of our need for perpetual renewal; where we see ourselves and want to turn away; where so many *do* turn away, that we find practical ways of embodying the Word of God, to the relief of those who feel themselves to be rejected, unloveable and unloved, fatally flawed and broken – their relief and great joy.

Epilogue

Mental Health Chaplaincy

The shape of psychiatric chaplaincy has changed radically during the last ten years because of the closing down of the huge old psychiatric hospitals. On the whole it has changed in the direction of greatly increased opportunity. Psychiatric Hospital Chaplains are now known as Mental Health Chaplains; whereas they used to concentrate upon the hospital itself, its patients and staff, they work outside nowadays, as members of the team which looks after people suffering from mental illness, some of them ex-patients of the old hospital, who now live in the neighbourhood, no longer inmates but ordinary citizens like everybody else. Except that they are ex-patients, and the neighbours would prefer them to move ... The work of these new chaplains is extremely varied. They are members of multi-disciplinary teams, which means that their activities are co-ordinated with those of doctors, nurses, social workers, clinical psychologists, occupational therapists and specialists in rehabilitation; although there are still acute and elderly chronic patients to care for in hospitals, they are needed in homes, both public and private, sheltered workshops, day centres, drop-in clubs, and every kind of place where patients and ex-patients are to be found; at the same time they are expected to work as liaison officers with local clergy in whose parishes ex-patients live, and congregations amongst whom ex-patients worship ...

Dealing with people's fear of mental illness and handicap is a principal part of his or her job. From one point of view mental health chaplains are ideally suited to do this because

of the links they have with congregations in the local neighbourhood and in the worldwide church. All kinds of contacts
may be made, from prayer companionships and special
relationships with a local church, to the provision of helpers
to transport patients to services or push wheelchairs. On the
other hand, by working in the old hospital and being closely
associated with it, the chaplain shares in the stigma which
attaches to it, binding him or her even closer to the people to
be served.

Psychiatric or Mental Health Chaplains occupy a special
position both within the health service and the church. Not
belonging to any large grouping, either in a hospital or in a
community health service, they can feel professionally isolated, so that they are grateful for the existence of the official
chaplaincy bodies, the Hospital Chaplains' Fellowship and
the College of Health Care Chaplains. Because they don't
work in parishes they tend to feel cut off from the normal life
of the church which goes on outside the walls. On the other
hand, their very strangeness gives them a kind of significance,
both in the health service and the church. Quite often they
are invited to speak to groups from local churches on the
subject of mental illness because of their specialist involvement – an important educational function which should not
be overlooked and could very well be developed more systematically by church districts, deaneries and dioceses. (I get
the impression that people like to hear about mental illness,
even though they may be terrified of coming into closer
contact with it; and anything that helps to erode the many
layers of myth surrounding it is surely to be encouraged.)

The singularity of the chaplain among the various 'power
groups' of the local health service also turns out to be even
more of an advantage. Because he or she is located outside
the professional hierarchy, she or he has access to every level
of it without disturbing protocol. In fact, by earning the
respect and affection of staff and patients, the chaplain can
rise to considerable heights within the unofficial hierarchy,

precisely because he or she is in touch with all sorts of people at every level of authority and 'has the ear of the hospital'. This kind of thing has to be earned, however. People must be able to trust the chaplain before they can use him or her to carry important messages they are too shy or timid to deliver themselves. The odd thing is that this privilege comes from the absence rather than the presence of power. It is because chaplains present no threat to anyone in terms of the structure on which employment depends that they can contribute in a unique way to the welfare of those they serve.

It seems to me that the chaplain does have power, therefore – but it is the power of another kind, the kind that is 'made perfect in weakness'. Chaplains have to be approachable and supportive, willing to listen and try to understand – above all, not on their clerical dignity. In the long run everything depends on personal relationships, and hence on love. In the competitive and defensive atmosphere of the Health Service, to discover somebody who is willing to listen to you without constituting any professional threat can be a source of considerable strength. Nowadays, with the proliferation of managerial functions and the strict delimitation of responsibilities attached to each, this is more difficult than it used to be. The shape of the organization keeps changing and the people one used to relate to now have other jobs to do. The scope of the chaplain's responsibility has also changed, but its essential nature remains the same, and will do so as long as chaplaincy remains a part of the service. As the service changes, the supportive and enabling role becomes more important than ever. An advertisement in this week's *Church Times* describes a job as a Mental Health Chaplain covering 'a range of psychiatric services including a Regional Secure Unit, academic areas, a nationally renowned therapeutic community and many other specialist areas,' with 'the opportunity to be involved with the rehabilitation, resettlement and continuing care of patients in the community'. The new chaplain will 'serve the needs of three major sites plus community settings, in co-operation with NHS staff, the churches, voluntary and other interested groups'. This is rather different from undertaking to provide spiritual and pastoral care for a particular psychiatric hospital and 'endeavouring to develop links with the neighbouring community'. Times are changing! The job, however, remains the same. The chaplain is called to fulfil a priestly and pastoral role in a particular situation. It is the setting that has changed, and confusingly so.

Appendix

The Closure of the Hospitals

The events surrounding the closure of the hospitals are a crucial part of many lives. Why did it happen? Why were these communities destroyed in the callous way that they were? Why take a living hospital and substitute a deserted barracks?

As long ago as 1983 Dr S. Winfield, writing in the MIND magazine *Open Mind*, expressed the same feeling of shock:

> Whatever reservations there are about ... Hospital, at least it exists. Its closure is a risky and experimental move, which should have been funded and planned accordingly. Instead it is to be run down before alternative services exist. The future of many psychiatrically disturbed people seems a grim one. Those who are more able, or have friends or family, will probably manage to obtain the help they need. Those less able will join the prison statistics or become vagrants, or perhaps just sit alone in a room somewhere ...

Dr Winfields's predictions have come true: they were bound to do so, so long as hospital closure was to take precedence over any provision for rehousing.

This is the crucial circumstance. Closing the hospitals just couldn't wait until there was somewhere else for the patients to go. This was the culmination of a policy which started in the mid-1950s aimed at closing psychiatric hospitals as rapidly as possible. There were two main reasons given for the urgency of the decision. First of all, it was stated that changes in the effectiveness of psychiatric treatment made long stays in hospital unnecessary. The new psychoactive drugs rendered the management of psychiatric illness much easier; disturbed patients could be pacified without physical restraint or actual surgery. It became possible to reduce the intensity of the symptoms of mental illness, although it was still not possible to cure it altogether. New non-medical approaches began to be used, with particular success in the treatment of phobics and the rehabilitation of institutionalized patients. It began to look as though it would be possible, by a combination of mood-changing drugs and sophisticated teaching methods, to train patients to earn their own discharge by learning to cope inside the hospital with some of the demands that would be made on them in the world outside the gates.

The second reason concerns society itself. During the 1950s and 1960s there was a growing volume of criticism over the use of psychiatric hospitals as a way of dealing with mental illness. A large amount of sociological research was devoted to examining the pathological effects of institutionalization. It was argued that these hospitals could not avoid being anti-therapeutic because of the structural rules governing their operation: 'total institutions', they created their own world which had little to do with normality. This was held to be true even if they did not abuse the patients in the ways that everyone believed they did. Living in 'a place like that' carried with it an unavoidable stigma. It was – and is – assumed that people who lived in an asylum must, of necessity, be mad; as long as the asylum remained, madness would have little chance of being assimilated into society like all other illnesses. Psychologists and psychiatrists pointed out that the feelings of stigma that prevented patients from having the courage to leave hospital were their own version of society's attitude towards them, for a person's experience of him or herself is affected by his or her own idea of the way he or she is regarded by others. In other words, by putting people into institutions you teach them to see themselves the way they think society sees them – as outcasts, rejects, lunatics. Thus, the problem was believed to be a psychological reaction to a social attitude: if the hospitals were knocked down, this would all vanish. Little regard was paid to the existence of actual mental illness, or to the fact that most symptoms occur before anyone has even thought about hospitalization. On the other hand, there is little doubt that hospitals like this exercised a good deal of their control over patients by manipulating the anti-social tendencies they existed to cure – childish over-dependency, self-indulgence, the wily ability to 'play the system'.

These are good reasons, but they are not the real reason. The real reason has to be a *very* good reason; one cannot imagine closing the hospitals down before making alternative provision for either of these reasons, which after all are both therapeutic, at least in the broad sense. The real reason is, of course, money. The origins of the present situation go back a long way. Mental hospitals owe their existence to a particular way of thinking about society, one which says that those 'who will not *or cannot*' work must be carefully segregated from the rest of the community, including those who are capable of working but have been allowed to become a burden on the economy by living off funds provided for poor relief within the community. In its desire to make sure that nobody received support who was not willing to work, a market economy had little time for the Elizabethan Poor Law; if money was to be spent on the poor and sick, this must happen within special institutions away from the workforce. Nowadays the most effective and the cheapest way of providing for the health of the workforce is by 'community care'. In the nineteenth century the state spent money on social outcasts while the community looked after itself. Nowadays, however, the situation is reversed. Now the community receives state relief and its outcasts must learn to conform. So far as the state is concerned, they are the wrong people, in the wrong place, at the wrong time. No modern state can afford to spend money on both kinds of people, particularly when the first are profitable and the others are not ... In our own case the mental hospitals are simply left to run down, while attention is concentrated upon kinds of welfare provision which will be available for people living at home. Unfortunately, however, psychiatric help comes far down the list. Ex-psychiatric hospital patients are caught between the devil and the deep blue sea.

Which is where you will find them. And the opportunities with them.

Glossary

Anxiety (Morbid) A feeling of fear or apprehension often accompanied by a disturbance of the nervous system, which is not caused by any particular situation but persists.

CPN Community Psychiatric Nurse – a nurse attached to General Practice, trained in the care of mentally ill and mentally handicapped people. CPNs receive referrals directly from anyone who is anxious about somebody's mental health.

Delirium A state which reflects a pathological condition of the brain; its symptoms are overactivity, illusions and disorientation.

Delusion A false belief, held in the face of logic, which is inappropriate to an individual's socio-cultural background. Delusions are often held with extraordinary conviction.

Dementia Progressive, irreversible intellectual impairment, caused by organic brain disease.

Depression Illness which concerns a person's mood. It resembles sadness or grief, but is more extreme in its effects and cannot be relieved by any kind of verbal persuasion.

Its symptoms are reduced by anti-depressant medication. It goes away of its own accord in time.

Group home

A household made up of ex-users. Group homes have been endowed by various charities and by local health and social service authorities. Typically, they accommodate four or six people who, in ideal circumstances, will have been given an opportunity to get used to living together before moving in.

Illusion

A perceptual error, commonly occurring in organic mental states such as delirium.

Neurosis

A state of cognitive and emotional unease which does not involve actual brain abnormality and in which contact with reality is maintained. Symptoms of distress are effectively relieved by medication (see *Psychosis*).

Obsessional State

Ideas and associated feelings of an unpleasant recurrent kind, resisted by someone (e.g. a person has to perform every action of washing nine times or else he or she becomes distressed).

Paranoia

A psychosis characterized by ideas that (i) other people are concentrating their efforts to do you ill; (ii) you yourself are immensely important. As a psychosis it loses touch with reality.

Phobias

Extreme anxiety linked to the presence of specific stresses (e.g. heights, open spaces, dogs etc) and only triggered off by these.

Psychosis

A condition of mental disorder in which contact with reality is lost, and the person believes that he or she is entirely sane. Although medication can prove very effective in reducing the symptoms, the condition does not actually refer to real changes in the brain.

Schizophrenia

A group of psychotic conditions in which the personality begins to disintegrate and people have difficulty in relating to others. It is often a condition of young people. It is not totally curable by medical means but people can often 'live through' it, and its symptoms are very greatly reduced by modern drugs.

Bibliography

1. Mentall Illness

Atkinson, J., *Schizophrenia at Home*, Croom Helm 1986.
    Practical and reassuring.
Beck, A. & Emery, L., *Anxiety Disorders and Phobias*, Basic Books 1985.
    A useful handbook.
Clare, A., *Psychiatry in Dissent*, Tavistock 1976.
    The most balanced book I know in a very controversial area, the nature and proper treatment of mental illness.
Foskett, J., *The Meaning of Madness*, SPCK 1985.
    Mentally disturbed people make more sense than is generally assumed, if you know how to listen to them. The author is a full-time psychiatric chaplain.
Laing, R. D., *The Divided Self*, Penguin 1965.
    Still, after all this time, a controversial book. For those who question the medical model of mental illness it suggests an alternative way of interpreting the evidence about schizophrenia. *See also*
Laing, R. D. & Esterson, A., *Sanity, Madness and The Family*, Penguin 1970.
Nicholson, J. & Lucas, M., *All in the Mind*, Methuen 1984.
    This is probably the book to read first, before attempting anything weightier.
Rowe, D., *The Successful Self*, Fontana 1988.
—, *Depression: The Way out of Your Prison*, Routledge 1983.
    Two books by a leading psychological specialist in depression. They represent a positive approach to a frightening subject.

2. Psychotherapy

Jacobs, M. (ed), *Faith or Fear*, Darton, Longman & Todd 1987.
A collection of readings exploring the relationship between religion and psychotherapy. Fascinating reading for those who want to dig deeper.

Storr, A., *The Art of Psychotherapy*, Secker & Warburg and Heinemann 1979.
Not an easy book for a beginner but well worth the struggle, as are all Dr Storr's books.

3. Learning Difficulties

Haverwas, S., *Suffering Presence*, T. & T. Clark 1988.
A book noted for its compassion and the depth of its reflections on handicap.

Vanier, J., *L'Arche*, Darton, Longman & Todd 1974.
Classic revelation of mental handicap.

4. Pastoral Work

Grainger, R., *Watching for Wings*, Darton, Longman & Todd 1979.
Theology and mental illness in a pastoral setting. This centres on chaplaincy in a large, old fashioned psychiatric hospital.

—, *A Place Like This*, Churchman 1984.
Impressionistic portraits of life in a psychiatric hospital. Meditations and prayers.

5. Health

Lambourne, R. A., *Community Church and Healing*, Arthur James 1987.
A seminal book. First published in 1963, it opened the way to modern Christian thinking about community.

Melinsky, M. A. H., Millard, D. W., Goodacre, D., *Religion and Medicine*, Vols 1–3, SCM Press 1970–76. Vol 4, IRM 1983.
Any of the volumes – indeed, any of the essays in these four books – is worth reading. Together they make up a concerted plea for understanding about health.

Pattison, Stephen, *Alive and Kicking*, SCM Press 1989.
A practical theology of illness and healing.
Wilson, M., *Health is for People*, Darton, Longman & Todd 1975.
An expressive work about the power of healing inside individuals and communities.

6. *Old Age*

Robb, B., *Sans Everything*, Nelson 1967.
A book about the bad old days that are only just over. Worth reading in order to see what we have left behind us.

Useful Organizations

Alzheimer's Disease Society

The society offers advice and support to families of sufferers and promotes care and research into Alzheimer's Disease. 150/160 Balham High Road, London SW12 7BN (071 675 6557–6550)

APCMI – The Association for the Pastoral Care of the Mentally Ill

This is an ecumenical organization seeking to enable Christians to undertake work with users and ex-users. There is a national organization which provides training, and local branches which vary in their function according to the needs of the area and the interests of the people involved. Apart from creating awareness at the local level of the plight of mentally ill people, APCMI aims at 'raising the consciousness' of those who have a say in the running of the churches at a national level. To this extent it is a pressure group in favour of user-liberation; people who suffer from, or have suffered from mental disorder should be allowed and encouraged to live life as fully as they can without the additional handicap of social marginalization, which exists whether the walls are visible or invisible. Visible walls, the physical presence of the hospital, defined community too rigidly. Invisible walls, however, are capable of imposing total isolation. At the local level it is a lifeline for hundreds of individuals who, however much they may have resented their patient status and felt restricted by it, were used to being at home in psychiatric hospitals and now find themselves at large in the world. It is also an essential means of support and advice for those who are actually ill, in the sense of being disturbed, and are having difficulty in gaining acceptance of the fact in the face of the quota system operating with regard to psychiatric beds. People who are disturbed may need a change of environment, somewhere to go until the crisis has passed. Their families certainly need this respite almost as much as they do. Nowadays it is difficult to get, particularly as a preventative measure. Only people who are at a critical stage of mental illness are admitted to hospital. This is the situation that APCMI confronts. Its aim is to give both users and their families the help they so desperately need. APCMI, 351 City Road, London EC1V 1LR (071 278 3438).

Campaign for People with Mental Handicap
A pressure group working for the rights of people with learning difficulties, based at 12A Madox Street, London W1R 9PL (071 491 0727).

The Churches' Council for Health and Healing
This is a kind of umbrella body bringing together a wide range of Christian groups dedicated to health and healing. Several mainstream Christian denominations are represented and advice about help for individual needs is available. It should be stressed, however, that this is primarily an information resource. The Churches' Council for Health and Healing, Marylebone Parish Church, Marylebone Road, London NW1 5LT.

Ex-Services Mental Welfare Society
The only organization specializing in helping those suffering from psychiatric disabilities who have served in the Armed Forces or Merchant Navy. Hollybush House, Hollybush by Ayr, Ayrshire (0292 56214).

The Manic Depressive Fellowship
The Fellowship is run by users themselves and has groups in many parts of the country. It is a good example of a self-help association, publishing its own magazine, *Pendulum*. Its headquarters is at 13 Rosslyn Road, Twickenham, Middlesex TW1 2AR (081 892 2811).

MENCAP – Royal Society for Mentally Handicapped Children and Adults
The Society aims to increase public awareness and understanding

of the problems of people with mental handicap (learning difficulties) so as to provide them with the conditions they need. MENCAP National Centre, 123 Golden Lane, London EC1Y 0RT (071 253 9433).

The Mental After-Care Association
This Association provides residential homes and hostels for adults recovering from mental illness in the South of England. Headquarters: Bainbridge House, Bainbridge Street, London WC1A 1HP (071 436 6194).

MIND – The National Association for Mental Health
The largest and most influential mental health association, formed to keep an eye on Health Service provision for mentally ill and mentally handicapped people. There is a local group in almost every town, and perhaps a drop-in centre or a hostel for ex-users. Groups are autonomous, being affiliated to central MIND, part of whose work consists in carrying out research, organizing conferences and preparing reports. MIND, 22 Harley Street, London W1N 2ED (071 637 0741).

Psychiatric Rehabilitation Association
This is a self-help organization pioneering residential care, day centres, industrial education units etc, in co-operation with men and women who have suffered long-term mental illness. Headquarters: 21A Kingsland High Street, London E8 (071 254 9753).

Richmond Fellowship
The Richmond Fellowship provides community care for people recovering from mental health problems. Founded in 1959, it has an excellent record. 'Thirty-two years of service have seen thousands of people go through Fellowship houses and make a good recovery,' by which is meant becoming as independent as they can. The Fellowship is a nation-wide organization – there are now more than 60 community facilities providing a range of support from intensive to minimal. In some places the Fellowship provides an advocacy service for those still living in hospital. The Richmond Fellowship, 8 Addison Road, London W14 8DL (071 603 6873–5).

Schizophrenia Association of Great Britain
Established to help people suffering from mental illness and provide
support for their families, particularly to promote research into
nutritional factors which may contribute to schizophrenia. Inter-
national Schizophrenia Centre, Bryn Hyfryd, The Crescent, Bangor,
Gwynnedd LL 57 2AG (0248 354048).